The Ultimate Guide
JEET KUNE DO

Editors of Black Belt

Graphic Design by John Bodine
Layout by Ghislain Viau
Cover Design by Sophea Khem

©2010 Cruz Bay Publishing, Inc.
All Rights Reserved
Printed in South Korea
Library of Congress Control Number: 2010908053
ISBN-10: 0-89750-186-1
ISBN-13: 978-0-89750-186-6

First Printing 2010

BLACK BELT BOOKS
A Division of **OHARA** PUBLICATIONS, INC.
World Leader in Martial Arts Publications

Table of Contents

Foreword

It should come as no surprise that Bruce Lee topped the list when *Black Belt* conducted a survey of the most influential martial artists of all time. Consider some of the things the "Little Dragon" did.

- The charisma and talent he demonstrated in his movies lured tens of thousands into martial arts schools. "Lee appealed to everybody," says *Black Belt* Hall of Fame member and former tournament champion Karen Sheperd. "Everyone, including me, wanted to emulate him. He impacted a lot of people."

- Lee's skill was phenomenal. He was incredibly fast, powerful and precise. Even today, 28 years after his death, people want to know how he trained. "My hands are faster today than they were before I met Bruce," says pressure-point expert George A. Dillman. "Bruce definitely influenced my speed. He made me faster."

- Lee is the guy who got the entire cross-training ball rolling. He was way ahead of his time ... to say the least.

- Through his movies, he made people more aware of the martial arts. "I think everybody watched Bruce Lee's movies," says film star and retired tournament champ Cynthia Rothrock. "He's the first one who really introduced the martial arts to the public. He's an icon."

- He developed *jeet kune do*. "He studied his art and developed a system that made a lot of sense to a lot of people," Sheperd says. "Furthermore, he was very scientific in his approach."

With accomplishments like those, it's no wonder Bruce Lee was featured on the cover of *Black Belt* so many times. And this is why we gladly dedicate this ultimate guide to his influential martial art.

—Editors of *Black Belt*

截 拳 道

Order Out of Jeet Kune Do Chaos:
The Key to Understanding
the Legacy of Bruce Lee

by Jerry Beasley, Ed.D. — January 2000

It is often said that while Bruce Lee was alive, he and his art of *jeet kune do* were at least 10 years ahead of the times. In the 1960s and early '70s, Lee's theories on combat were considered by many to be of the highest level. It took most of the martial arts community a decade to understand his insightful writings. Now, more than 26 years after his death, we realize that some fighters eventually—and perhaps independently—arrived at similar conclusions without ever referring to Lee's work. The observation could be made, for example, that the winners of no-holds-barred fighting events are shedding an identification with the limitations of style as they reach a level that Lee may have originally envisioned when he created jeet kune do.

One has to believe that if Lee had lived, he would take great pleasure in observing NHB fighting events. He would also be equally amused by the various "faces" his art now wears. By all accounts, there are at least four clearly discernible groups that offer a slightly altered interpretation of jeet kune do, and each group seems to have its own agenda. That is not a bad thing; it simply gives testimony to the lasting importance of Lee's views on the martial arts.

The four "faces" of *jeet kune do* can be classified as original, eclectic, concept and strategies. Pictured above: Tim Tackett (1), Dan Inosanto (2), Jerry Beasley (3) and Paul Vunak (4).

Academically trained in philosophy and sociology, I have over the years sought to understand JKD's philosophical puzzles as I observed the formation of group behaviors. Depending on whom you ask, JKD is described in various ways. I believe there is only one JKD, and it is so simple to understand that it is easily confused or mistaken for different arts or interpretations. For this reason, JKD can be said to wear four faces.

In this article, I will examine the philosophy of JKD and identify the four interpretations (faces) that separate and identify it. My conclusions represent no single view and are not meant to oppose any other interpretation. For several years, I have taught a class on JKD at Radford University in Virginia. The students—who are on their way to earning a degree in psychology, philosophy, science or some other field and who represent various martial arts—enjoy engaging in heated debates over the philosophical merits of Lee's classic text *Tao of Jeet Kune Do*. Many of the ideas I will present in this article were bred in the classroom and tested on the mat, in the ring and on the street. When it comes to interpreting JKD, I have absorbed what was useful; now I give back what is uniquely my own.

To require dedication from students and, of course, to amuse those who could read between the lines, Lee often disguised simple meaning with philosophically meandering phrases. Forgive me if I, too, occasionally use Bruce Lee-inspired philosophical musings to illustrate that which is all too apparent. I am reminded of the Bruce Lee movie *Circle of Iron*. Toward the end of it, Cord, the seeker, opens the book of knowledge and begins to laugh. The knowledge he had so laboriously sought, he already knew. I hope some martial artists will read this article and, perhaps for the first time, experience the joy of discovering that which they may recognize as their own. JKD is about discovering that which we already know in a manner that sets us free to understand the totality of our endeavors.

Liberation From the Known

To understand JKD, we must seek to comprehend the totality of combat. Without taking a position of contention, we must observe each path along the way. Enlightenment can be achieved only when we are free to see JKD. If we are burdened by preconceived limitations brought on by personal prejudice or peer pressure, then seeing JKD becomes—as Lee said—not unlike mistaking a finger pointing at the moon for heavenly glory.

Let's suppose that three martial artists from different styles witness a fight. Upon returning to their respective schools, the *taekwondo* expert tells his students about the excellent kicks. The judo expert explains to her class that grappling skills won the fight. And the boxer notes that upper-body strikes were among the most significant techniques of the fight. In general, we expect practitioners of different styles to demonstrate an individual preference for specific strategies and tactics.

Rather than letting us stay in our own comfort zone and dissect the fight into easy-to-understand arts or skills, JKD philosophy requires that we examine the big picture. JKD is not about style but about results. The way we "see" the fight is a good indication of our limitations. In JKD, we often use the expression "using no way as way" to mean that we do not focus on the way the fight is to be won or the art that is used to prevail.

JKD was never completed. What Lee developed can be called a conceptual framework. A conceptual framework may be likened to a lens in a pair of eyeglasses. If the lens is red, the images we see will have a rosy tint. Lee's lenses—the way he visualized the martial arts—were composed of the concepts and values he accumulated and applied to his personal understanding of the fighting arts.

We know, for example, that Lee preferred arts that could justify "economy of motion." He stressed reality in training. We also know that he valued arts not for their cultural origins but for their utility in the combat arena. To him, arts were of value only when they could be used in grappling, kicking, punching and trapping ranges. As a result of the various NHB fighting championships, I have often written that the classification of range may be more appropriately referred to as kickboxing, trapboxing and ground submissions.

Lee's conceptual framework varies considerably from the conceptual framework of a karate or taekwondo master, a kung fu champion or a grappling expert. Each person carries unique preferences, values and concepts that reflect his own interpretation of what he prefers in a martial art. Lee researched a variety of arts for the sole purpose of extracting any method or technique that could be adapted to his personal strategy for fighting. He may have practiced *wing chun* kung fu, but when it was reorganized and transformed through his conceptual framework, it no longer closely resembled wing chun.

Imagine going to a food store with a shopping list of the items needed to cook spaghetti. You quickly survey a number of canned goods, produce, pasta and other items and select only the ingredients needed for that recipe. The world of the martial arts became Lee's "shopping center." From his selection of arts, he coordinated a variety of skills into his personal JKD matrix: the techniques he could apply with authority at any fighting range. In the end, the skills he performed—his JKD—did not represent any of the arts he had originally studied. He was free of all arts; he was JKD, liberated from the known.

Obviously, few of us have the ability or desire to gain freedom from all arts. In fact, we often pride ourselves in our identification with one or more arts. We tend to accumulate knowledge rather than continually refine our thinking by chipping away the nonessentials. The quest for knowledge may indeed lead us to many paths, but how often do we find ourselves going in circles?

What is the way to JKD? We must let experience be our primary guide. We must involve ourselves in combat in its many forms. We must learn to kick with a master kicker, box with an accomplished boxer and go to the mat with a champion grappler. We must discover for ourselves what really works and what is only "style baggage."

Unlike in other systems, the student of JKD is best advised to study under several teachers. Each should be a master of his preferred fighting range. Good advice for acquiring skill in JKD is to seek not to specialize but to find our place at the particular moment to understand the totality. To express JKD, we must be able to draw from the totality of all we have learned or accomplished without preference.

To respond like an echo, we cannot be burdened by style. To use no way as way, our technique must be refined to a point by having no exact line. We simply "repose in the nothing," having no limitation as limitation. How do we accomplish these things? If we know nothing about the martial arts, we are already there. Yet we must train and advance. As we train, we follow the path toward JKD. The journey is longer for some than for others, and there are a few shortcuts. But to find the artless art—the art of the soul at peace, as Lee would call it—we must be prepared for a different way of thinking. We must empty our cup.

JKD is a destination that can be reached by many paths. It is at once clear to the eye, then it is void. It is like a mirage that is perfectly in view yet cannot be touched. Why? Because it is an experience of total freedom. When we become conscious that we are JKD, we lose our focus on the moment and return to the realities of self-imposed limitation. But it is always worth the effort.

One Art, Four Ways

JKD is freedom from all styles. As we become JKD, we must understand the meaning of formlessness and using no way as way. The goal of JKD is to float in totality. Rather than use a predetermined self-defense form, we must learn to simply respond with economy of motion. JKD is a philosophy of attaining liberation from all systems of classical thought and, as such, leaves much room for interpretation.

Is JKD a style? Yes and no. From 1967 until 1973, Lee taught JKD sometimes as a style (1967-71) and sometimes as a way of surpassing styles. The first face of JKD can be called the "original art." People who follow this way view it as a style. The terms "original art" and *Jun Fan* are used to identify the goal of those who seek to discover and understand JKD as an identifiable art replete with specific skills, training routines and a close identification with the founder.

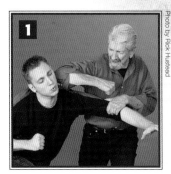

Because Lee died at age 32 without having designated a master or inheritor, we must use the word "interpretation" when we refer to various systems that are called JKD. When Lee was alive, JKD was variously referred to as "Bruce Lee's art," Jun Fan kickboxing, scientific street fighting and nonclassical *gung fu*.

When I received my first black belt in 1971, I vividly remember that many people in the martial arts community referred to Lee's nonclassical gung fu as full-contact kickboxing. Joe Lewis had introduced the American art of kickboxing in 1970, so that term was often applied to any art that used boxing gloves and karate kicks. In fact, the characteristic that best described JKD was that the practitioners engaged in full-contact sparring with protective equipment. The equipment included boxing headgear, a baseball umpire-style chest protector, boxing gloves or exposed-fingertip *kenpo* gloves, and baseball-style shin protectors with sneakers.

Lewis, who was the best fighter ever to train with Lee, introduced the JKD principles of economy of motion, weapon-first movement and the five ways of attack to martial arts tournaments as early as 1968. At about this same time, an interesting phenomenon took place: A new system called American karate was gaining a tremendous following. It used as its premier concept the JKD principle of using the best from all arts. Over the years, many martial artists who never actually practiced JKD began to feel comfortable using the term "jeet kune do" to identify any system that promotes the best from each style or advocates using what works.

JKD students are best advised to train under several different teachers. Pictured above: Jerry Poteet (1), Lamar Davis (2), Ted Wong (3) and Joe Lewis (4).

A second interpretation of Lee's brainchild can be called "eclectic JKD." This view is perhaps the dominant interpretation worldwide. Eclectic-JKD groups have formed in Europe, Asia, South America and North America. Most practitioners are simply karate school members who incorporate the "using what works" terminology and utilize JKD practice methods such as contact sparring.

By recognizing eclectic JKD, our intention is not necessarily to give credence to that interpretation but simply to state that thousands of practitioners fall into that category. Most would consider those devotees to be on the fringe of the JKD community, but they constitute a major force in the practice of the Bruce Lee methodology.

A third group is formed by those who practice "JKD concepts." With its base of multicultural martial arts, it is perhaps the most popular interpretation. Following Lee's original research methods, JKD-concepts practitioners attempt to establish a common thread while linking several arts, depending on the functional range or fighting distance of the confrontation.

A fourth view, which can be called "JKD strategies," holds that the plan of action is of primary importance. JKD-strategies adherents blend the skills of the original art with continued research and development. Staying true to the theme of using no way as way, they refuse to be limited to any single art (including original JKD) or group of arts (as in the JKD-concepts method). They view JKD as a synergy, with the end result being greater than the sum of the parts. While several arts must be studied, no single art or way dictates the strategy to win.

Conclusions

Those are the four faces of JKD: the original art, eclectic JKD, JKD concepts and JKD strategies. Each interpretation appears different and, according to some proponents, should exist at the exclusion of all others. Still, in a way, each interpretation is related to the Bruce Lee legacy. Will all JKD practitioners eventually join together into a single group? Not likely. To be JKD is to be not bound by traditional rules or conventional styles.

It is important to understand that as soon as we deny the utility of one interpretation, we begin to establish rules and boundaries for our own expression of the art. Limitations negate the validity of JKD.

Certainly, it would simplify matters if we could just agree that jeet kune do refers to only the art taught and practiced by Bruce Lee between 1967 and 1973. Any other interpretation would have to be called "JKD plus"—or, as noted above, JKD strategies, JKD concepts or eclectic JKD. Lee, however, claimed he did not create a new art; rather, he established a method to free us from all arts. Thus, any attempt to say JKD is only this and never that would be, in his own words, incorrect.

It is important to understand that Lee initiated a concept—using no way as way—that has led to a number of new and valid ways of defining self-defense. True, JKD continues to experience growing pains as it seeks to identify a solitary expression from the multifaceted complexity that exists in the martial arts. And regardless of which face we currently see, JKD, once experienced, has the synergistic vitality to assist us in actualizing a genesis of new potential in the combat arena.

截 拳 道

Slippery as a Snake:
The Elusive Lead of
Bruce Lee's Jeet Kune Do

by William Holland — January 2001

Bruce Lee belongs to that select group of martial artists who accomplished so much during their life that they changed the way the world fought. Although part of his success stemmed from his phenomenal physique and rapid reflexes, much of it was because of the highly effective tools and techniques he chose to focus on. One of them was the "elusive lead."

Strong-Side Lead

Lee bucked convention when he insisted that your strong arm be put in the lead (or forward) position. Although that may seem unconventional to boxers and traditional martial artists, weapons systems such as fencing and *kali* apply the strong-side-lead concept quite successfully.

What are the advantages of the strong-side lead? For one, it puts your strongest weapon closer to your opponent, enabling it to be used more frequently. Because it is your dominant hand, it is probably more accurate, quick, powerful and coordinated; and because it is your strong side, you can generate more natural power

Bruce Lee took the concept of the strong hand forward from Western fencing.

without having to use as much body movement. Thus, your jab and lead hooks can be deployed with quick and devastating results while you maintain economy and simplicity of motion.

That Lee held the lead punch in the highest regard is evidenced by a passage from his *Tao of Jeet Kune Do:* "The leading straight punch is the backbone of all punching in *jeet kune do*. It is used as an offensive and defensive weapon to stop and intercept an opponent's complex attack at a moment's notice. The leading straight punch is the fastest of all punches. With minimum movements involved in delivery, balance is not disturbed and, because it goes straight toward the target, it has a better chance of landing."

Longest Weapon, Nearest Target

When attacking or intercepting, the JKD fighter predominantly uses punches to the upper body and head while keeping kicks confined to the midsection and below. When attacking, he often strikes with his lead hand or foot while parrying with his rear hand. That maintains the economy and directness of the lead punch by not entangling those lead tools for defensive purposes. This fighting principle is called "using the longest weapon to attack the nearest target."

In JKD, defense is often employed with shifting and evasive footwork and body movement, slipping and bobbing rather than blocking or making contact with the opponent's weapon. When contact is made, it is often done with a light parrying motion with the rear hand. That keeps the lead hand out of the line of engagement and free to hit the unsuspecting opponent.

Serpent's Tongue

In addition to maintaining a constantly shifting body and head, Lee advocated keeping the lead hand in a state of motion. Darting in and out like the tongue of a snake, your lead hand can be used with quick, broken rhythm to upset the opponent's timing, confusing him or inducing him briefly into a trancelike state.

This movement also provides momentum before a lead punch or strike—somewhat like having a running start at the beginning of a race. Known as the "hammer principle," this moving start works like a stone skipping off a lake, with the punch picking up speed and rotation as it ricochets off an imaginary wall.

The movement of the serpent's tongue should be crisp and economical, moving in and out, up and down, worrying and bothering the eyes and timing of the adversary. As he watches the quick movements of your lead hand, that hand can be used to fake or open avenues for your rear hand and other weapons.

Felt Before It Is Seen

By constantly moving your lead hand, you have the advantage of what Lee called "choice reaction." In other words, by watching not only your flicking lead hand but also your shifting body, the opponent must analyze and choose how to respond to various potentially dangerous stimuli, thereby slowing his reaction time.

Unlike many classical styles of fighting, JKD emphasizes not having a set posture or stance. With your lead hand constantly moving and your feet and body shifting continually, you must be able to strike at any time from wherever your hand happens to be. You should be able to execute the strike without assuming a position of power. You should practice striking with your lead hand in motion, from various positions or gates, and immediately after a fake or parry without chambering it.

Lead vs. Counterpunchers

The elusive lead is a superb tactic to employ against a counterpuncher. Not only does the elusiveness of the strike make it difficult for him to time and predict your entry, but the technique also incorporates a varying of the defensive positions of your head and limbs.

While changing the position of your lead hand before the delivery of a strike, you should also vary the position of your head, rear hand, body and returning hand when you attack. That will upset his intentions.

For extra precaution against that type of fighter, you can also change the position of your rear guarding hand as well as the position to which you return your lead hand. If you do so, he will have no clue where your head or hands are. That will further interrupt his game plan.

Angular Attacks

In JKD, much weight is given to striking directly and efficiently in a straight line because it is the shortest distance between two points. However, a skilled opponent will know this, too, and will strive to take the direct line away. Thus, the elusive lead is used to strike along a straight line when it is available and along a curved line when it is necessary.

Depending on the defensive positions of the opponent's guard, you may at one moment use a straight blast to the centerline and at another moment use a backfist, corkscrew hook or low-line jab to avoid his defensive tools and strike his most vulnerable target.

With your lead hand constantly moving, you should be able to deploy these various strikes from assorted positions of transition. For instance, if the opponent is standing in a left lead and leaves his left temple exposed, you can deliver, from a right lead, a right corkscrew jab from a low position, high position, centerline position, outer-gate position, and inner- or outer-perimeter position—all while moving.

Progressive Indirect Attacks

Another primary tactic of JKD is the progressive indirect attack. You use your lead hand or foot to initiate the attack, and when the opponent moves his guard to defend, your lead hand continues at a divergent angle to strike the newly exposed target.

Whereas many fighters fake with one weapon and score with a different one, the progressive indirect attack uses the same weapon to create the opening and then immediately strike it. That is particularly advantageous because your lead weapon is already halfway to the target.

With the power and economic explosiveness learned from the one- and three-inch floating punch, you can unload a tremendous amount of torque and penetration with a minimal amount of movement or muscular effort. So while the progressive indirect attack travels a relatively short distance from the transition point of the feint, your entire body unloads with whiplike speed to inflict a lot of pain and damage.

In all strikes, your weapon should be deployed before the rest of your body, thereby saving the maximum amount of rotation and power for the moment of impact. The movement of your hips, torso, legs and shoulders is unleashed just as your weapon makes contact; it allows the payload of power from your body to be dumped on the opponent's body and not wasted en route.

As Lee wrote in *Tao of Jeet Kune Do*, "You never strike your opponent with your fist only; you strike him with your whole body." To try to muscle up and hit with a lot of muscular force from your arm is like trying to throw a nail into a board. It is more efficient to place the nail (your fist) onto the target and apply force with the hammer (your legs, hips and torso).

Doubling Up

A "re-doublement" is two rapid consecutive blows to the same target with the same weapon. It can be very fruitful against a fighter who merely leans away or slips his head slightly to avoid your first jab or strike. He leaves his guard down or out of the line of attack because he believes that a simple evasive move will be sufficient. Because his defensive guard is not obstructing your line of attack, another strike on the same line coupled with an advancing step can drive your second blow through the target. Often, a fighter who leans or slips away immediately will return his head to its original position, thereby increasing the impact of your second strike.

Another type of fighter who lends himself to being hit with the re-doublement is the one who quickly parries your first blow but takes his parrying hand back away from the attack line, thereby exposing the line for your follow-up hit. You can penetrate the small crevice he creates by pulling his parrying hand away with the re-doublement because his attacking hand does not return all the way back to its original position, striking instead from half to three-quarters of a recoil.

Ricochet Hit

When confronted by a skilled defender who does not open himself up to the re-doublement, you can try another proven elusive-lead tactic: the "ricochet hit." It is similar to the re-doublement in that it uses lead-hand strikes in rapid succession. The difference is that you use a different angle, level or target with the second blow. Examples include a lead jab-lead hook combination, a low jab-high backfist combination and a lead backfist-lead ridgehand combination.

Progressive lead attacks divert an opponent's attention with a feint. Here, the JKD practitioner (left) feints with a low straight lead punch before hooking to the opponent's head (1-3).

Photos by Thomas Sanders

The ricochet hit is similar to the progressive indirect attack in that the same weapon is used twice; however, the first movement must be meant to score and not merely to act as a feint. As Lee was fond of saying: When in doubt, hit.

As the defender gets hit by parries and blocks or evades your initial backfist, he may inadvertently expose the other side of his head to a ridgehand or hook. If you drive a penetrating low jab into his ribs, his reaction to getting hit or his attempt to keep from getting hit may cause him to lower his guard and expose himself to a quick backfist. The key to making the ricochet hit succeed is ensuring that the initial strike places your lead hand in close proximity to him, thereby reducing the distance and travel time.

Cutting Edge

The elusive lead can take your fighting skill to a higher level. When using it, keep the following principles in mind:

- Remain loose and relaxed with crisp, shifting movements.
- Make each strike brief and explosive between longer periods of relaxation.
- Be predictably unpredictable.
- Use movement and body torque, not the swinging force of your arm, to supply the power.
- Let your hand be the nail and your body be the hammer.
- Hit like a bullwhip, not like a ball and chain.
- Be able to strike at any time, to any target, from any position, at any angle.

截 拳 道

Bruce Lee and Sun Tzu:
The Founder of Jeet Kune Do Was a
Devout Follower of The Art of War

by Matthew J. Numrich — March 2001

T o grow as a martial artist, you must constantly find new sources for learning. One particularly valuable source for practitioners of all styles is Sun Tzu's *The Art of War*. Written almost 2,500 years ago, the book was created as a guide to winning on the battlefield. Since then, numerous scholars have analyzed it—translating, interpreting and theorizing about its true meaning. Many have also related its concepts to 21st-century life and personal growth.

As the owner of a personal-growth company, I was at first curious about the "success content" of *The Art of War*. Although I discovered that it offers many useful concepts and insights, its message pulled more at my other profession: teaching Bruce Lee's *jeet kune do*. I found it amazing that a manuscript written around 500 B.C. could relate not only to modern military operations but also to plain old-fashioned street fighting.

This article will offer some insights into the correlation between *The Art of War* and Lee's theories, which include his jeet kune do philosophy.

One

The first chapter of Sun Tzu's classic is titled "Laying Plans." In Lee's opinion, it is essential to have a plan for every contingency of combat. That's why he divided fighting into the four ranges: kicking, punching, trapping and grappling. In a typical fight, he would inflict pain from a distance, enter and follow up at close range.

Having a plan also applies to training. It pays to have a game plan for preparing your body to implement the skills you learn. Without the proper physical foundation, knowing all the fighting techniques in the world will not do you any good, Lee said.

Two

The second chapter is titled "Waging War." It teaches you to pick your altercations wisely and take advantage of proper timing.

Sun Tzu wrote about the importance of the terrain in military maneuvers; martial artists can interpret that as being able to defend themselves in different environments and on unfamiliar surfaces.

"The value of time—that is, being a little ahead of your opponent—has counted for more than … numerical superiority," Sun Tzu wrote.

Lee concurred: "By obtaining an edge of speed on the adversary, [you] may lead him. In other words, it is the adversary who continually will have to try to catch up. If [you] have a sufficient margin of speed on hand, it is possible to maintain this advantage. To do so [you] must have a moral effect on the opponent who, finding himself subjected to [your] will, cannot fail to suffer in his confidence."

Sun Tzu also wrote, "Cleverness has never been associated with long delays." Or with long fights, Lee might have added.

Three

The text's third chapter, "The Sheathed Sword," has a psychological focus. Sun Tzu wrote, "To fight and conquer in all your battles is not supreme excellence; supreme

Recommended Resources

The Art of War is available in numerous versions, each of which has comments and insights provided by its editor. I prefer James Clavell's edition from Delta Business. It is short and to the point. While other editors have given Sun Tzu's book a more lengthy and in-depth treatment, Clavell sticks mostly to the raw text so you can ponder the author's views.

Bruce Lee's *Tao of Jeet Kune Do* has been a best-seller since it was first printed in 1975. —MJN excellence consists of breaking the enemy's resistance without fighting."

In other words, if you can end an altercation without resorting to violence, you are the supreme tactician. Lee demonstrated one version of this strategy in *Enter the Dragon* when he was challenged by one of the martial artists who were being ferried to Han's island. Instead of fighting the other man then and there, Lee persuaded him to do battle on a smaller vessel that was being towed behind the larger boat. Once the challenger boarded the dinghy, however, Lee untied it from the mooring, leaving the feisty fighter alone on the craft.

The third chapter of *The Art of War* ends with this bit of wisdom: "If you know the enemy and know yourself, you need not fear the result of 100 battles. If you know neither the enemy nor yourself, you will succumb in every battle."

Lee devoted several pages of his *Tao of Jeet Kune Do* to a discussion of the value of self-knowledge. "Understanding yourself happens through a process of relationships and not through isolation," he wrote. "To know yourself is to study yourself in action with another person."

Four

The fourth chapter is titled "Tactics." It relates to knowledge. "One may know how to conquer without being able to do it," Sun Tzu wrote. Lee had the same idea in mind when he wrote, "Knowing is not enough."

Sun Tzu advised people "to plan secretly, to move surreptitiously, to foil the enemy's intentions and balk at his schemes." JKD practitioners are taught to fight the same way: "If a fighter concentrates sufficiently, senses the moment to attack and acts upon it swiftly and decisively, the prospects of success are greatly enhanced," Lee wrote.

A variety of attacks were deemed essential by Sun Tzu and Bruce Lee. The pictures illustrate striking, kicking and grappling arts (1-3).

Five

"Energy" is the title of the fifth chapter. Upon reading it, JKD practitioners will be reminded of *hubud*, *chi sao* and *sumbrada*, all of which are common energy drills.

I believe the chapter also relates to momentum, which is a form of energy. When combined with lines of attack, momentum is one of the most important

Photos courtesy of Matthew J. Numrich

After studying their writings, it becomes apparent that Bruce Lee and Sun Tzu agreed on many things, including the effectiveness of feints in combat. To illustrate, Matthew Numrich (right) fakes a low kick to make his opponent react (1). Numrich then punches high (2). Next, Numrich initiates a high punch (3). But when the opponent responds, Numrich kicks low (4).

principles of fighting because it allows you to feint. While feinting, you quickly find out that different lines of attack exist. These progressive indirect attacks, as Lee called them, teach you how to use the feint to open up even the most skilled opponent.

Sun Tzu stated, "In all fighting, the direct method may be used for joining battle, but indirect methods will be needed in order to secure victory." Similarly, Lee wrote: "There is little direct attack in jeet kune do. Practically all offensive action is indirect, coming after a feint or taking the form of countering after an opponent's attack is foiled or spent."

Six

The next chapter, "Weak Points and Strong," illustrates the importance of adaptation. Being able to adapt to a ground fight, mass attack, weapons altercation or battle that moves from long range to close quarters is one of a JKD practitioner's greatest assets.

When Lee wrote, "Be flexible so you can change with change," he was in agreement with Sun Tzu's thoughts: "He who can modify his tactics in relation to his opponent and thereby succeed in winning, may be called a heaven-born captain."

This refers not only to modifying the physical but also to modifying the emotional. If you keep the same physical and emotional dispositions in trapping range as in grappling range, Lee taught, you will lose. You must change to meet the combative challenge of the moment.

Seven

The seventh chapter is titled "Maneuvering." It teaches that in any altercation, movement dictates success. "Let your rapidity be that of the wind, your compactness that of the forest," Sun Tzu wrote. "In raiding and plundering, be like fire; in immovability like a mountain."

Lee is said to have spent hours studying film footage of boxing greats like Muhammad Ali to analyze how they maneuvered. He concluded: "[You should] always keep [yourself] just out of distance of the opponent's attack and wait for an opportunity to close the distance or to steal a march on the opponent's advance. Back him to a wall to cut off his retreat or retreat yourself to draw an advance."

Lee added: "Moving is used as a means of defense, a means of deception, a means of securing proper distance and a means of conserving energy. The essence of fighting is the art of moving."

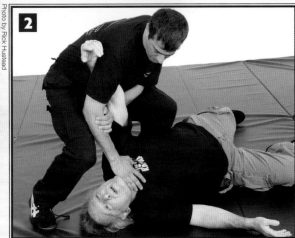

Sun Tzu's use of the term "fire" can be translated into the *jeet kune do* concept of "killer instinct:" A martial artist should do whatever it takes to defeat an attacker—even if his response seems barbaric (1-3).

Eight

In the eighth chapter, "Variation of Tactics," Sun Tzu showed how to intelligently choose targets. Victory can be had by confusing your opponent's defense with a variety of offenses, he wrote.

Beginning JKD students are often advised to master a few key moves, but advanced practitioners are told to seek added variety. For example, it is good if you perfect the eye jab for self-defense, but you should also have other tools in your arsenal: groin kicks, thigh kicks, oblique kicks, low-line punches, toe jabs and so on.

Lee designed the JKD fighting stance so the practitioner could access a variety of tools. "The on-guard position is that position most favorable to the mechanical execution of all the total techniques and skills," he wrote in *Tao of Jeet Kune Do*.

Nine

Sun Tzu's ninth chapter, "The Army on the March," deals with the preface of a fight. You must use your powers of observation and intuition to discern your opponent's physical, mental and emotional disposition to create the most efficient line of attack, he advised.

Lee identified the first stage of an altercation as an assessment of the opponent (often called the probing stage). When describing the psychological process of attack, he wrote that step No. 1, the survey, "is entirely mental and can be divided into two parts: definable (the estimation of the correct distance between the fighters or the appearance of an opening), and instinctive (whether the opponent will attack or retire). During this phase, [you] decide how to attack."

Ten

The most important lines from the 10th chapter,

"Terrain," are: "The natural formation of the county is the soldier's best ally; but a power of estimating the adversary, of controlling the forces of victory, and of shrewdly calculating difficulties, dangers and distance, constitutes the test of a great general. He who knows these things, and in fighting puts his knowledge into practice, will win his battles."

JKD practitioners call this principle "using the environment." Lee taught that it is one of the most important aspects of realistic self-defense.

Eleven

The 11th chapter is titled "The Nine Situations." It explains the types of "ground" a soldier may encounter. Sun Tzu listed everything from facile ground to open ground to ground of intersecting highways. His descriptions parallel descriptions of the environment in which a modern martial artist could find himself.

Two additional items can be found in this chapter. The first is: "Rapidity is the essence of war. Take advantage of the enemy's lack of preparation, make your way by unexpected routes and attack unguarded spots." The second is, "By altering his arrangements and changing his plans, the skillful general keeps the enemy without definite knowledge."

Both passages relate to adapting, which Lee thought was crucial to success. He realized that a practitioner must be able to adapt to any range and use any weapon. "A good man steals, creates and changes the vital spatial relations to the confusion of his opponent," he wrote.

Twelve

The 12th chapter, "Attack by Fire," explains how the flame can function almost as a secret weapon. Sun Tzu's references to fire bring to mind the secret weapon of JKD: killer instinct.

Sun Tzu wrote, "In order to carry out an attack with fire, we must have the means available." The same holds true with killer instinct: You must have it nearby and be able to switch it on like a light the moment it is needed.

Lee wrote: "The attitude, 'You can win if you want to badly enough,' means that the will to win is constant. No amount of punishment, no amount of effort, no condition is too tough to take in order to win. Such an attitude can be developed only if winning is closely tied to [your] ideals and dreams."

Thirteen

The Art of War concludes with "The Use of Spies." Sun Tzu wrote, "What enables the wise sovereign and the good general to strike and conquer, and achieve things beyond the reach of ordinary men, is foreknowledge."

That is not to imply that Lee spied on other arts or practitioners. Rather, he learned from them. Many of today's leading JKD instructors have continued to evolve. It is not uncommon to see modern interpretations of Lee's art incorporate teachings from *kali*, Brazilian *jiu-jitsu* and other styles; that is one reason it has stayed on the cutting edge.

"Jeet kune do favors formlessness so that it can assume all forms; and since jeet kune do has no style, it can fit in with all styles," Lee wrote. "As a result, jeet kune do utilizes all ways and is bound by none and, likewise, uses any technique or means which serves its end."

Epilogue

The Art of War shows itself to be not only timeless but also very useful in numerous facets of life. Even 2,500 years later, its teachings still hold true.

The art of war is more of a process than a product—much like JKD. I cannot help but think that if they had been contemporaries, Bruce Lee and Sun Tzu would have had a lot to talk about.

截 拳 道

Legacy of Bruce Lee:
Dan Inosanto Strives to Keep the Art and Philosophy of Jeet Kune Do Alive

by Floyd Burk — November 2001

J*eet kune do* is one of the martial arts' most precious jewels, and its adherents are among the most skilled practitioners in the world. They train in an environment that helps them develop spontaneous and deceptive combat skills with an emphasis on adaptability. JKD is all about action: moving, shifting, kicking, punching, trapping, blocking and parrying. It is a continuum of perpetual motion, yet there is a flow of stillness that encapsulates awareness, perceptiveness and intuition.

Nearly 30 years have passed since JKD's creator, Bruce Lee, made his final bow, leaving a remarkable legacy to his students and his students' students. When he died, the torch was passed, and ever since, JKD has been guided by his foremost disciple: Dan Inosanto.

The Los Angeles-based Inosanto has gone the distance to preserve and spread Lee's art and philosophy. And when it comes to inspiring martial artists to open their minds and embrace those teachings, Inosanto has accomplished more than most. Why are there so many loyal JKD practitioners? "Because Inosanto is educated, warmhearted and sincere," says *tai mantis* kung fu master Rob Moses,

Attitude Adjustment

As Dan Inosanto travels the world spreading the gospel of *jeet kune do,* he gets a good sense of the changing attitudes of 21ˢᵗ-century martial artists. "People are much more polite now," he says. "People are much more courteous, more open to learning things that are not part of their discipline and more appreciative of other arts. I think that's important because as Bruce Lee said when he pushed *gung fu,* 'If they can appreciate a Chinese martial art, maybe they can appreciate the Chinese culture.' And if they can appreciate the Chinese culture, they can appreciate other Asian cultures. If they can appreciate Asian cultures, they can appreciate African cultures, European cultures and Middle Eastern cultures. Understanding other cultures will help [achieve] world peace." —F.B.

who was one of David Carradine's instructors. "He extends open arms and invites other schools and styles into his academy. The welcome mat is put down for everyone all over the world. Inosanto is such a blessing to the martial arts—who wouldn't want to be part of it?"

Despite the art's popularity, people are still confused about JKD and its roots: *Jun Fan gung fu* and *wing chun.* And the mystery of how Lee would have wanted his art to evolve remains unsolved. Nevertheless, learning how Inosanto's personal expression of JKD has changed over the years is sure to shed new light on this great art.

Foundation

Lee appended the given portion of his Chinese name, Lee Jun Fan, to the Cantonese pronunciation of the term "kung fu" to devise a name for the institutes he opened: Jun Fan Gung Fu. That also became the name of what resulted when he combined wing chun with Western boxing, added some footwork and *savate* techniques, and spiced it all up with his own discoveries.

After conducting additional research and sprinkling in some essential principles, strategies and concepts, Lee transformed Jun Fan gung fu into an entity he named "jeet kune do." Whereas Jun Fan gung fu was a set system, JKD was a philosophy and an ongoing process of self-discovery. It represented his personal exploration and the path he followed for self-perfection by way of meditation, spiritual training and martial arts. It is well-known that as soon as he thought up the name, he regretted it because boundaries and limitations would be set on his principles and ideals. And boundaries and limitations are not part of JKD.

After Lee died, Inosanto had to figure out how to carry on without the master. To keep things as he believed Lee would have wanted, Inosanto decided to continue using the curriculum Lee devised for Jun Fan gung fu and make it the foundation on which students could build their understanding of JKD's advanced components and eventually make it their own expression. "When we say Jun Fan gung fu, we mean the original art that Bruce Lee handed down," Inosanto says. "But when we say jeet kune do, that's our personal growth. Jeet kune do, as Bruce Lee said, cannot be standardized, but it can be taught."

Dan Inosanto (right) faces Erik Paulson (1). Inosanto feints low (2) before striking high, but the opponent stops the attack (3). Inosanto counters by firing a lead-leg kick into the other man's groin (4). He then follows with an eye jab (5), a trap (6) and a backfist (7).

The thing that sets Inosanto apart from many other Bruce Lee followers is that he participated in the development of Jun Fan gung fu and JKD. A meticulous record keeper, Inosanto was a schoolteacher who taught English, social studies and physical education at the secondary-school and college level. He helped Lee organize things and introduced him to different training tools. Because Inosanto had an extensive background in *kenpo*, weapons and other arts, he could help Lee in the creation and coining of different JKD methods and terms.

Basics

In Jun Fan gung fu, the basic stances include the natural stance (the position in which you're standing when you are attacked) and the fighting stance. The fighting stance is similar to that of boxing, except that the feet are a bit more than shoulder-width apart, the toes are turned inward and the heels are raised. The hands begin at 10 o'clock and 2 o'clock, but they move constantly. "The [positioning] in itself is just a moment in time because when people try to classify it, they miss the idea because it's in a constant flow," Inosanto says. "It's like taking a picture of a football player when he's on the field. The hands and feet constantly move. The key thing on stance is to have mobility and stability."

One thing Inosanto has instituted—and one that is different from the way Lee taught—is the need to be symmetrical. In other words, students learn how to do their techniques from a left-hand lead and a right-hand lead. The logic behind that policy is that even if one part of their body is taken out of action, they can continue to fight.

Inosanto still teaches simultaneous attack and defense, but there are times when it cannot be used, he says. He doesn't emphasize blocking as much as some instructors do, but he does block and cover during the execution of hook punches and similar techniques. "We don't over-block," he cautions. "Sometimes it's good just to move your body. There's a time to do the heavy parry and the heavy block, but it's usually very light. [For defense], it's light parries to move out of the line [of attack], slipping, bobbing and weaving."

Evolution

Inosanto believes that to survive, martial artists need a good stand-up game, a good off-balancing game, a good ground game and a good weapons game. They must be multidimensional.

"We use pretty much the same kicks that Bruce Lee handed down, but I would say kicking has evolved in a subtle way that is taking place even now," he says. "When I was training with Bruce Lee, we used a lot of side kicking, low side kicking and angling of the side kick. [Now], we go more with hook kicks and

Dan Inosanto (left) and his opponent face each other (1). The opponent punches, and Inosanto deflects the blow as he uses his lead leg to kick the other man's lead leg (2). The *jeet kune do* expert then shifts forward to execute an eye strike (3). The opponent pushes away the attacking arm (4), but Inosanto traps his arm (5) and delivers a punch to his nose (6).

round kicks. We use material that's similar to *muay Thai*. You can block with the kicks, and you can obstruct with the kicks. We did this before muay Thai, but muay Thai has added to our understanding. So have *bando* and savate. They added more. More doesn't mean better, but more gives you an understanding of more types of attacks."

Always on the cutting edge of martial arts development, Inosanto also recognized the need to add modern ground fighting and submission training to his academy's curriculum. Consequently, Brazilian *jiu-jitsu* and shootwrestling classes are taught in conjunction with the Jun Fan gung fu classes. "The people that are in jeet kune do have adapted into learning how to survive on the ground," he says. "Most of them have at least trained in shootwrestling, Brazilian jiu-jitsu, Greco-Roman or some kind of freestyle wrestling to balance themselves. I like to have all my students exposed to shootwrestling because it is a very good art and will make them more well-rounded. Some people go more into the savate, and that's good, too. It's like when you go to a Chinese restaurant and they have 30 to 100 dishes. Your dishes will always be different from your friend's dishes because you are eating what you like. The martial arts are the same way."

Inosanto is a talented weapons instructor, and *kali* and other Philippine weapons arts play a big part in what he teaches. "People don't [always] want to learn weaponry," he says. "But 80 to 95 percent of all confrontations on the street involve a weapon, either blunt or bladed. If you have no training with a weapon, you won't even have a clue about how to defend yourself."

Adaptability

"Bruce Lee used to give me a quote from *The Art of War:* 'People are very intelligent at knowing themselves but ignorant at knowing others.' Why isn't it vice versa?" Inosanto asks. "Jeet kune do is about being multidimensional. If a person is not multidimensional, he cannot really function in the year 2001. In the 1950s, style went against style, and everybody punched the same. But nowadays people strike differently, they attack differently. Some people are grapplers, some are strikers, and some are a combination. The structure that fit so well in one decade may not be the structure you would use in the next decade."

Consider military tactics. Although George Washington triumphed over the British at Valley Forge, Inosanto says, no modern army would choose to use the exact same methods Washington used. That's why Lee said the JKD practitioner must be adaptable. "However, you have to start someplace," Inosanto says. "A person doesn't just become adaptable. He needs a structure, and the structure Lee gave it was Jun Fan gung fu."

Inosanto is a hands-on kind of guy who likes to train with different people, and that sort of experimentation is also a hallmark of JKD. "Even if you think what you know is superior, sometimes the progression [other martial artists] use might be good," he says. "Or the procedure they use for a move might be good."

If a particular fighting strategy doesn't work against a sparring partner, it doesn't mean the strategy is unworkable, Inosanto continues. "You may learn four or five ways to counter a hook, but you may still get hit with the hook. It doesn't mean the technique is inferior; it's just that you've got to work on your own attributes, your own timing, your own positioning. I always liked a saying my mother gave me: 'A failure is the fire that tempers the steel, thus producing a fine product.'

You need the setbacks. Setbacks make you want to learn. Bruce Lee was correct when he said, 'It's from the old that you have security, but it's from the new that you grow and learn to adapt.' "

Truth

Every system hands down what it calls truths, but sometimes those truths may not be the truth for you. No two people fight exactly the same way, Inosanto says, because fighting includes an emotional element, an attitude. "If you're more aggressive, you may go straight in," he says. "If you're more on the passive side, you can be very efficient backing off.

"It was [Arthur Schopenhauer] who said truth passes through three stages, and I'll just paraphrase: The first stage is that it is ridiculed, the second stage is that it is violently opposed, and the third stage is that it [is accepted as self-evident]—there was never a question about it."

A prime example of those attitudes toward truth can be found in Inosanto's recollections of the mid-1960s. Lee began to advocate cross-training—both in other martial arts and in other athletic endeavors. For example, he said bicycling, swimming, weight training, dancing, gymnastics and yoga could benefit a person's martial arts practice. And he asserted that training in a grappling system would help a striker and that training in a kicking system would help a puncher. "When Bruce Lee advocated cross-training, it was ridiculed; it was violently opposed," Inosanto says. "Now if you read any magazine, the thing to do is cross-train. Now it is accepted as being always true, the thing you should have done."

Conclusion

Despite being afloat in a sea of JKD instructors, Dan Inosanto stands out like a lighthouse. One of the reasons is he continues to teach the original curriculum that Lee set, allowing each student to absorb what is useful and peel away what is not. And he never let himself get bogged down by the name "jeet kune do" or catch phrases such as "using no way as way" or "the truth is outside all fixed patterns."

We Are the Champions

Ever wonder why you never hear about JKD champions?

"Jeet kune do people do compete, but they do not compete in jeet kune do," says *Black Belt* Hall of Fame member Dan Inosanto. "They compete in Brazilian *jiu-jitsu,* shootwrestling, *muay* Thai and *savate.* But they don't enter under jeet kune do. Some people would be shocked because it is only supposed to be for street survival, but I encourage it."

"There are a lot of champions," Inosanto continues. "In the earlier years, we used to have California Golden Gloves champions. We've had several muay Thai champions, and there are many who've competed in stick fighting and won world championships." —F.B.

Dan Inosanto (left) and Erik Paulson square off (1). Inosanto strikes high to elicit a reaction from his opponent (2), then exploits the opening by kicking low (3). The *jeet kune do* instructor attacks the opponent's eyes (4) before thrusting his fingers into his neck (5) and blasting his elbow into his jaw (6).

Rather than inventing hidden meanings or explaining what Lee meant, Inosanto lets the founder's philosophy stand on its own. He encourages people to think for themselves and draw their own conclusions. He also brings other martial arts and artists into the spirit of JKD by teaching them to investigate, experiment and improve themselves. He continues to teach Bruce Lee's art as a method of self-discovery, and tens of thousands of his followers believe that is the loftiest goal of martial arts training.

截 拳 道

4 Keys to Jeet Kune Do:
Learn the Essential Attributes and
Proven Ways to Develop Them!

by Paul Vunak — 2001

Since the passing of Bruce Lee in 1973, we have heard many people try to define *jeet kune do*. Inevitably, when the descriptions vary, we hear these same people argue over whose definition is more accurate. Trying to label JKD is much like trying to define religion; the topic is far too subjective for it to be an easy task.

Adding to this confusion are the sometimes cryptic notes Lee left behind. Attempting to decipher his philosophy without actually having experienced each quote can be daunting. Imagine a non-martial artist reading the phrase "using no way as way, having no limitation for limitation." These words are simply too ambiguous for the linear logic of the Western mind. In my opinion, Lee's *Tao of Jeet Kune Do* is best read bit by bit. I just open the book, and whatever page I happen to land on, I read. I've studied JKD for 24 years, and every time I pick up the *Tao*, I still learn something new. That is why I believe that rather than trying to create a concrete answer as to what JKD is, it is more helpful to choose certain qualities that set it apart from other styles.

In this article, I have done just that. The four aspects that I believe differentiate JKD from everything else are adaptability, aliveness, speed and economy of motion. In the following paragraphs, I will clarify the meaning of each one and explain how to develop it.

Defining Adaptability

To adapt in a street fight literally means to "flow" with the circumstances. Most martial arts have a particular way of fighting. For example, if you are a *taekwondo* stylist, your way is predominantly kicking; if you're a boxer, your way is predominantly punching; and if you're a grappler, your way is ground fighting. It's important to understand that street fights mutate and that you must be able to adapt to each mutation.

For example, a fight could start as a one-on-one altercation with you and your opponent standing. Then one person takes you to the ground, and it is now a ground fight. Another person could jump in, and you would be in a two-on-one fight. If two more people enter into the equation, you will be in a three-on-two situation. At this point, someone might grab a pipe, changing it into a weapons fight. In retaliation, someone else may grab a blade, making it a knife fight. The potential mutations are endless.

Keeping that in mind, it becomes obvious that the average martial artist, who is confined to only one way, could find himself in deep trouble. What if you are a boxer and wind up on the ground? Or you are a ground fighter in a crowded nightclub and you have to fight three people at once? Or perhaps you're a weapons expert but you have no weapon?

It is easy to understand why Lee valued the ability to fight in all ranges, to fight with weapons and to deal with a mass attack. This is truly what he meant when he said you must be like water and adapt.

Developing Adaptability

Adaptability means having the wherewithal to go from situation to situation without breaking the flow. It has been said that you will fight the way you train. The best drill for teaching someone how to adapt from event to event while fighting is simply to do it: Begin by sparring on your feet. You and your opponent have a rubber knife tucked into your belt and two sticks in your hands. As you move and spar with the double sticks, try dropping one stick and continuing in single-stick mode. Keep sparring with a single stick for about 30 seconds, then throw your stick away and begin knife sparring. Go about 30 seconds, then throw your knife down and kickbox. After kickboxing for 30 seconds, execute a takedown and grapple. Continue on the mat for 30 seconds, look for a way to create space, get to your feet and do one more round of kickboxing.

Such a progression represents real fighting because no street fight goes the way you expect. Sometimes your weapon slips out of your hand, you get knocked to the ground or you get up from the ground as your opponent does. You have to flow to survive.

Defining Aliveness

The term "aliveness" refers to constant or continuous movement. The traditional martial artist has a tendency to favor stability over agility. That is why karate and kung fu teach so many stances. Much of that stance training stems from tradition: In the old days, martial artists sometimes fought in boats and rafts. As the craft rocked, the practitioner would lose his base. Therefore, a low stance was deemed necessary.

Another reason was the terrain. If a martial art happened to develop in a country with exceptional rainfall, many of the altercations that took place there would have been on slippery ground. Again, a low stance was necessary to stay upright.

As the years passed, those particular styles failed to change with the times, and modern practitioners still adopt those low stances for use against boxers or street fighters in metropolitan areas. That simply does not work.

When fighting an opponent who is "alive," agility is preferred over stability. That is why Lee was such an advocate of Western boxing. He spent hours viewing fighters with exceptional footwork—such as Muhammad Ali and Sugar Ray Robinson. Lee believed that to hit with economy of motion and power without telegraphing, you need to know the footwork of boxing. When you are on your toes, sticking and moving, you can readily throw fakes and use broken rhythm and half-beats more easily.

Many martial artists have a predominant way of attacking and defending. But the JKD stylist adapts based on the fighting situation. Pictured are the styles of karate, Western boxing and Brazilian jiu-jitsu (1-3).

Photos by Rick Hustead

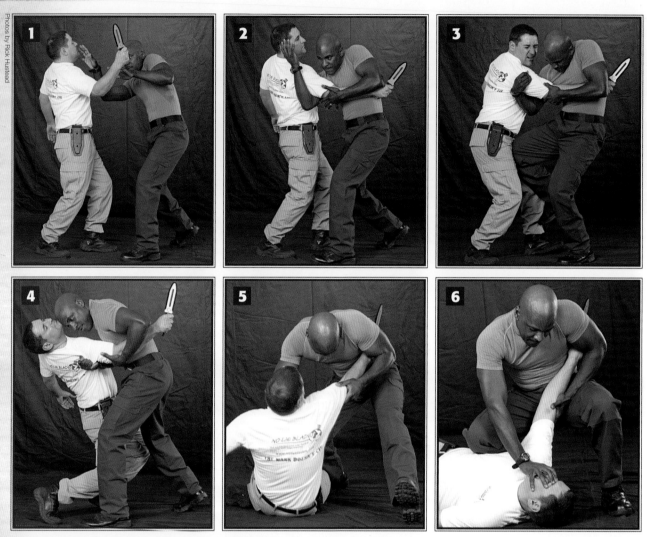

Street combat is full of variables, which is why the JKD practitioner wants to develop "aliveness." Here, Hank Hayes (right) blocks a knife attack to the eyes (1). Hayes then wraps his left arm over the man's right arm and secures it from underneath using his own right arm (2). He follows up with a knee thrust to the groin (3) and a head butt to the face (4). The finish begins with a takedown (5) and ends with a neutralizing eye strike (6).

When you apply those elements—footwork, timing, broken rhythm and half-beats—you can attack efficiently and viciously while making yourself an elusive target. That is the true definition of aliveness.

Developing Aliveness

A great drill for getting you on your toes—and busy—is knife sparring. When a *kali* practitioner spars with a knife, 90 percent of his time is spent aiming for his opponent's hand. That encourages the practitioner to be light on his feet and constantly moving.

On the other hand, if you and your opponent are kickboxing, you will have a tendency to "load up" and get planted so you can execute punches and kicks with maximum power. But when someone is wielding a razor-sharp knife, there is no need for power; the emphasis shifts to aliveness.

Defining Speed

Although I do not believe that speed is a prerequisite to being a good fighter, it would be negligent not to include it as an attribute that is an integral part of Lee's creation. After all, it is painfully clear how awesome his speed was, and to this day, the fastest man I have ever seen and the one who nearly set a record in the 100-yard dash (9.4 seconds) is Dan Inosanto, Lee's protégé.

To understand speed, you must first understand that there are different kinds of it. To define speed as simply "miles per hour" is akin to saying that Michael Jordan is simply "coordinated." As simple as the word sounds, you need to have a rather complex definition of speed. Think of it as the ability to close the gap between yourself and your opponent with explosiveness and economy of motion. As any physics major will tell you, power is directly proportional to mass and velocity. A small piece of lead thrown at a person can inflict pain. If the same piece of lead is hurled by a slingshot, it will inflict damage. If, however, it is propelled by gunpowder, it will cause instant destruction. The only factor that differentiates pain from destruction is the speed at which the projectile moves.

Although some people possess an inherent ability to be fast, it is possible to improve your speed without the gift of genetics. Nor does age automatically slow a person down. At 85, John LaCoste could wield a kali stick so quickly that the naked eye could barely see it move. And at 86, Helio Gracie can still get to your back and choke you out before you've counted your first sheep.

Developing Speed

Select a motion or technique you would like to execute more rapidly, then break it into two parts. For example, you can break the jab into part one, which is your hand extending outward, and part two, which is your hand retracting. Next, practice only the first part over and over. That develops your explosiveness, or as Lee used to say, your "suddenness."

This method works with virtually any martial arts technique.

Defining Economy of Motion

One of the most important attributes in JKD and one of the most difficult to convey, economy of motion is not how fast you move; it is how quickly you get to the target.

For example, if you have a fast jab yet tend to pull your fist back six inches before hitting the target, your fist doesn't actually get there that quickly. Conversely, if you execute a jab in a precise way following a direct line to the target without telegraphing your move, your fist will impact much sooner.

Another important aspect of economy of motion involves where you place your hands before punching. If you chamber your hands on your hips and are preparing to do a *wing chun* straight blast, it is impossible to move with economy of motion. Wing chun practitioners, who are known for their superior economy of motion, prefer to hold their hands near their centerline, and they never retract their fist before they launch it forward.

Developing Economy of Motion

One of the best ways to learn how to deliver a punch or kick without retracting your weapon first is to get into a stance and have your partner tie a string around your wrist. Step about three feet away while tightening up any slack on the string. Then attempt to execute the strike from that position. In the beginning, you may find that you yank the string right out of your partner's hand; that means you are moving backward before you move forward. Ninety-five percent of all martial artists have this bad habit, yet they have no clue that they are doing it.

Never-Ending Quest

Remember that JKD is composed of more than 30 attributes. In this article, I have simply chosen four that I believe stand out the most. It is also important to understand that these attributes are not exclusive to jeet kune do and that other styles also possess them to varying degrees.

Attributes are immutable. No one art, style, philosophy or ideology has a monopoly on them. Attributes transcend not only every martial art but also every activity in life. Bruce Lee summed up the whole concept when he said, "Man himself is more important than any established style or system."

截 拳 道

Jeet Kune Do Hands:
First-Generation Student Richard Bustillo
Explains 4 Combat Combinations That
Would Have Made Bruce Lee Proud!

by John Thomas Bingham — August 2002

Ever since it opened its doors in Carson, California, the IMB Academy has existed on the cutting edge of the martial arts. Because it was founded by two of Bruce Lee's most prominent disciples, it was able to offer the public the most effective and authentic *jeet kune do* training in the world. It eventually became one of those hallowed establishments—like the Kodokan in Tokyo, Kukkiwon in Korea and Shaolin Temple in China—at which the average martial artist can only dream about training.

Most of the fame associated with the IMB Academy, whose name stands for International Martial Arts and Boxing, grew from the tireless efforts of Richard Bustillo, a man who has devoted much of his life to preserving and propagating the timeless teachings of Bruce Lee. Bustillo was one of the "Little Dragon's" first followers in Los Angeles, and he was partly responsible for training Lee's children in the martial arts.

Although Bustillo, who was *Black Belt's* 1989 Co-Instructor of the Year, can trace his martial beginnings back to a nondescript Hawaii judo club he joined when he was 10, he has also trained in boxing, *kajukenbo*, *kali*, Thai boxing, wrestling, *jujutsu*, *silat* and, most recently, *tai chi chuan*. Yet he never lost sight of Lee's message, which is embodied in his jeet kune do.

"When I was 24, I met Bruce Lee, and I studied with him at the original Chinatown school," Bustillo says. "I was one of the original students there. Bruce emphasized the importance of being well-rounded in all ranges, and now at the IMB Academy, we focus on that concept. We like to use weapons in long range, boxing strikes and kicking in middle range, and grappling and trapping up close. You have to know all those ranges to be successful in self-defense."

To help readers become as successful as possible in their self-defense training, Bustillo decided to share the following four defensive techniques, all of which

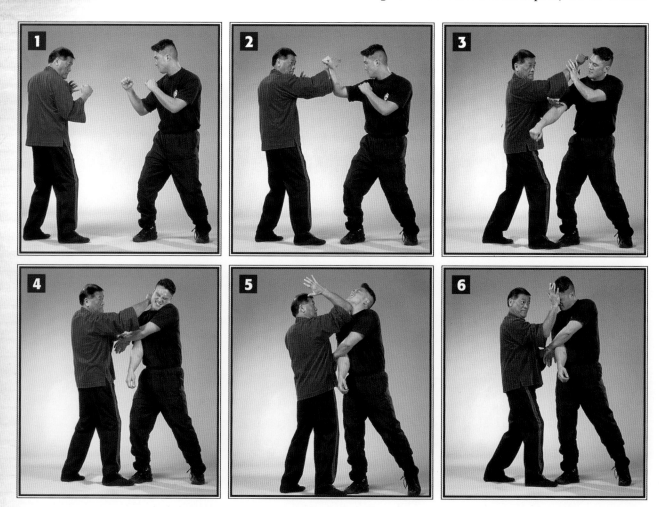

HAMMERING AWAY: Richard Bustillo (left) faces his opponent (1). He feeds a right hammerfist to him, and the opponent responds with a right-hand block (2). Bustillo executes a second hammerfist, and the opponent blocks it, as well (3). The *jeet kune do* expert then pulls the opponent's left arm across his body and lands a right hammerfist on his jaw (4). He follows up with an elbow to the chin (5) and a palm heel to the nose (6).

depend on JKD concepts and strategies. "Jeet kune do didn't include kali or *muay* Thai, but it does allow the individual to [create] his own curriculum," he says. "Although Bruce Lee never did the sticks or the leg blocks, the IMB Academy program does because the techniques work well for self-defense."

Hammering Away

You face your opponent in a right-hand-lead stance, which positions your strong side forward, Bustillo says. "You feed him a right hammerfist, which draws his right hand into blocking. You then trap his right hand with your left hand and attempt to strike with a second hammerfist, but he blocks it with his left hand."

To bypass his defenses, you execute a *lap sao*, in which you pull his left hand across his body, thus tying up both arms. "Then you can successfully land your hammerfist on the third try," Bustillo says. "And with his hands still trapped, you immediately execute an upward elbow to the chin, then drive the heel of your palm into the bridge of his nose."

Such a punishing combination is appropriate only in dire circumstances, Bustillo says. "Because a hit to the bridge of the nose or temple can do severe damage," he says, "you should do things like that only to stop aggression toward you—but you must stop the attacker as quickly as you can.

"When you're trying to execute this sequence against a dangerous opponent, you must have confidence so you can be fluid and quick. Try not to let him upset your flow or destroy any of the techniques, but if something should happen, you just have to adapt to the new situation."

Kick Interception

The next JKD response begins with you and your opponent standing in a left-leg-lead stance. He attacks with a lead-leg front kick, which you intercept by thrusting your left hand into his closest shoulder, thus disrupting his momentum. At the same time, you avoid what's left of his kick and trap his foot to keep him off-balance, Bustillo says.

"Once you get the kick, you step to your left so your left leg is positioned behind his right leg," he says. "Then you slide your foot and sweep him to the floor. Once he's down, you hook his left ankle with your right arm. Your left hand checks his knee as your right hand locks onto your left wrist."

You can finish the encounter at this point by executing an Achilles lock on his left leg. Alternatively, you can turn him onto his stomach, using your right foot to push against his butt for added rotational power. "Then you step across his back with your right leg," Bustillo says. "Once he's on his stomach, you exert pressure against his ankle and knee."

KICK INTERCEPTION: The opponent (right) prepares to assault Richard Bustillo (1). He launches a lead-leg front kick, and Bustillo drives his left hand into his shoulder before the technique is finished. He simultaneously moves off-line and traps the leg (2). Next, Bustillo slides to his left and places his left foot behind the other man's supporting foot (3). He then sweeps him to the floor and positions his arms for an Achilles lock (4). If he decides further restraint is needed, Bustillo can roll the opponent onto his stomach (5) and apply pressure to his ankle and knee (6).

FROM THE CLINCH: Richard Bustillo (left) ties up with his opponent (1). He uses his left hand to push the other man's right elbow across his throat (2), then steps to the opponent's right and uses his right arm to trap the arm in place (3). Bustillo plants his right hand on his left biceps and places his right hand on the opponent's head for a carotid choke (4). If necessary, the *jeet kune do* instructor can drive a knee thrust into the opponent's solar plexus to soften him up for the choke (5).

One possible drawback to using this JKD-inspired response is that you have to expose your body to your opponent in order to accept and trap his kick, Bustillo says. "You have to be skilled and confident enough to jam his left shoulder to prevent the kick from coming in at full strength."

From the Clinch

The next JKD response to aggression is designed to be used from the clinch, a frequently encountered standing-grappling position. Your right hand is cupped around the back of his neck, and your left is resting on his right arm. "Your left hand shoves his right elbow across the front of his throat," Bustillo says. "You then step to his right and bend your right arm to lock his right arm between his neck and your shoulder."

Next, you place your left hand on top of his head and lock your right hand onto your left biceps. That completes the figure-4 lock that constricts the flow of blood to his brain. "You can submit him from this position using the carotid choke, or you can add a knee thrust to the solar plexus," Bustillo says. "The knee strike takes away his balance and shocks his system. It lets you choke him more easily. If you try to go right to the choke, a lot of times he can defend himself or counter it, so you may have to take those options away by shocking his system.

"Normally, you don't want to get into a grappling situation on the street, but if

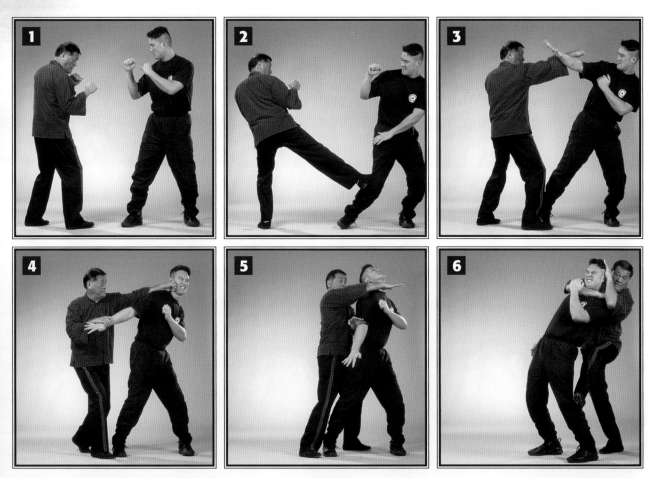

SET THE TRAP: Richard Bustillo (left) and his opponent face each other (1). As soon as the opponent begins to move, Bustillo stops him with a foot obstruction (2). He then advances and executes a hammerfist, but the opponent blocks it (3). Bustillo immediately yanks his blocking arm and slams a straight punch into the other man's face (4). Next, he pushes the trapped arm down, moves to the opponent's back and wraps his right arm around his neck (5). He finishes by locking on a rear-naked choke and kicking the opponent's left leg to destroy his base (6).

Although *kali* was not a part of Bruce Lee's *jeet kune do*, modern authorities like Richard Bustillo (left) include it in their curriculum because the movements it teaches translate to empty-hand self-defense.

you're in this position, you can execute a technique such as this one," he says. "It's still risky because the energy can change at anytime. You have to be able to adapt and possibly switch to some other technique. You should always have options."

Set the Trap

Bustillo's final defensive sequence works by laying a trap for your opponent. You slowly approach him until he is about to launch a kicking attack. "As soon as he moves, you stop him with a foot obstruction directed at the knee of his lead leg," he says. "When you put your kicking foot down and step forward, you have

41

to be careful because he can hit you with a punch or a hammerfist. If he strikes, you should block it with your right arm. If he doesn't immediately attack, you should strike to get him to block with his right arm. Once the two of you get to that position, you collapse it by using your right hand to pull his right arm as you execute a straight punch with your left."

Next, you reposition your left arm so your hand forces his trapped (right) arm downward. You should simultaneously close the distance between your body and his and encircle his neck with your left arm. The rear-naked choke is completed when you lock your right hand on your left biceps and your left hand on his head. Then, if you need to take him to the ground, you can drive your left foot into the back of his left leg, destroying his support system. His leg will buckle, and you will still have him immobile in the choke. He will have two options: submit or be rendered unconscious.

截 拳 道

5 Ways of Attack:
Rethinking Bruce Lee's Hidden
Meaning to Find the Truth in Combat

by Jerry Beasley, Ed.D. — September 2002

I t is well-documented that Bruce Lee taught different ideas about the martial arts during different phases of his personal development. Consequently, his methods are often categorized as being associated with the Seattle phase, the Oakland phase or the Los Angeles/Chinatown phase of his evolution. Also, it is generally understood that his private students often received instruction that differed from what was offered in the Chinatown classes typically led by teaching assistant Dan Inosanto.

Because of the variations that existed under the name of *jeet kune do*, it was important for each original student to compare notes with the others. Likewise, it is important for today's students of JKD to collect as much information as possible before arriving at any conclusions.

These days, it is popular to separate JKD into two branches: the conceptual school and the historically correct school. The conceptual school is often identified by a shift to Philippine and Indonesian arts, while the historically correct school has created the perception that it has neither altered nor deleted any of Lee's original skills. One writer has referred to the concepts school as "modern JKD"

In traditional *jeet kune do* instruction, attack by drawing is taught as a method of counterfighting in which the martial artist (left) "draws in" the opponent by creating an opening (1-2), then attempts to beat him to the punch. The problem, of course, is that the opponent may be faster (3).

(because those associated with it constantly update and advance their knowledge of JKD concepts) and the historically correct school as "traditional JKD" (because of the emphasis on staying true to Lee's chosen skills).

The differences between the two schools have resulted in many differences of opinion, but both sides seem to agree on the meaning and interpretation of Lee's five ways of attack: single direct attack, attack by drawing, attack by combination, hand (and leg) immobilization attack and progressive indirect attack. In light of recent research, however, there may be a previously uncovered interpretation of the five ways of attack that is far more advanced.

Once again, it is necessary to remind the reader that because of the unique nature of JKD, Lee was constantly transforming his research and development process. Therefore, it is understandable that his students differ in their interpretations of what they were taught and what they believed to be JKD. I don't wish to imply that any person's interpretation is superior to anyone else's. Rather, the goal is to point out that even the five ways of attack—which are the same for the concepts school and the historically correct school—are open to interpretation.

Attack by Drawing

There are no changes in the interpretation of the single direct attack or the hand (or leg) immobilization attack. However, the meanings of attack by combination, attack by drawing and progressive indirect attack need to be reconsidered. For example, attack by combination is traditionally thought to be a combination of single direct attacks. The boxer using a jab, cross and hook is a typical combination. In fact, attack by combination can be more effectively viewed as a combination of any two *ways* of attack—and not limited to only combinations of the single direct attack.

The real problem is not attack by combination; rather, it is the potential misinterpretation and commonly used limitations of attack by drawing. Traditionally, attack by drawing has been interpreted and taught as drawing in the opponent's attack by creating a false opening—a method of baiting the opponent. The opponent sees the opening and attacks. Attack by drawing (as baiting) is thus actually employed as a method of counterattack. If you follow this view, the five ways of attack become four ways of attack and one way of counterattack. Imagine that you decided to hunt sharks. If you subscribe to the

Photos by Lora Gordon

In *Jun Fan* kickboxing, attack by drawing refers to the art of drawing the opponent "out" through the use of fakes. To illustrate, Jerry Beasley (left) forces his opponent to react to a fake round kick (1-2), which creates an opening for a front kick (3-4).

Again using the strategy of attack by drawing, Jerry Beasley (right) fakes a lead-hand punch (1-2), which "draws out" the opponent's defense and creates an opening for a front kick (3-4).

traditional JKD interpretation of attack by drawing, you would dive into the water and wait until a shark attacks. That method is called "bait and wait." Exposing a target to attack is not generally recommended.

Apparently, the word "drawing" was thought of as only "drawing in." There is, however, a better way of drawing. In many old Westerns, when the good guys are penned in, one man always volunteers to move to a better position if his partners will draw the attacker's fire. They shoot at the bad guys to redirect their attention, thus allowing the volunteer to sneak away. While his friends fake an attack, the good guy uses an appropriate version of attack by drawing to win.

So what's the solution? Attack by drawing should be interpreted as both drawing *in* the opponent's fire toward a false opening (the traditional interpretation) and drawing *out* the opponent's fire by faking. If you fake a high punch and your opponent responds by attempting a block/parry, you have successfully employed attack by drawing as a method for drawing out an attack. As such, it is a method of offensively approaching the opponent.

There is, however, another problem. Traditionally in JKD, faking has been used as an element of the progressive indirect attack. So the student would no doubt be confused. Faking, when viewed as the art of creating a false attack that solicits an anticipated defensive reaction from the opponent, is more appropriately used in attack by drawing.

Progressive Indirect Attack

The progressive indirect attack requires a change in speed, direction or timing. A fake does not qualify as one because it is a completed technique. A progressive indirect attack must originate as an incomplete technique that changes direction or speed to find completion.

The term "broken rhythm" is most appropriately applied to the progressive indirect attack. To accomplish it, you disrupt your opponent's fighting rhythm by creating a misdirection or variation in speed. While it is a somewhat sophisticated method when compared to attack by drawing or single direct attack, it is nevertheless a common approach for beginners. Quite often, they have a natural broken rhythm that is seen as awkward. It is awkward enough to evade, but when employed by an expert, broken rhythm is even more difficult to defend against.

JKD Kickboxing Approach

While JKD has been referred to as Bruce Lee's jeet kune do, nonclassical *gung fu* and *Jun Fan* kickboxing, the kickboxing approach seems to be the most simplified venue for realizing it. In Jun Fan kickboxing, the fighters begin a process of eliminating all unnecessary skills as they focus on the five ways of attack. It is through this method that we can discover the revised uses of those five ways.

With sufficient contact-fighting experience, the Jun Fan kickboxer comes to realize that the proper execution of a single technique is considerably more important than the potential follow-up. Ultimately, the goal becomes that of educating the fighter in the simplest and most economical ways of attack.

Even though the Jun Fan kickboxer may employ only a few skills, he has at his disposal an infinite variety of ways to execute those skills in a decisive and effective manner. Former Professional Karate Association world champion Joe Lewis, who was voted the greatest fighter of all time in a 1983 *Karate Illustrated*

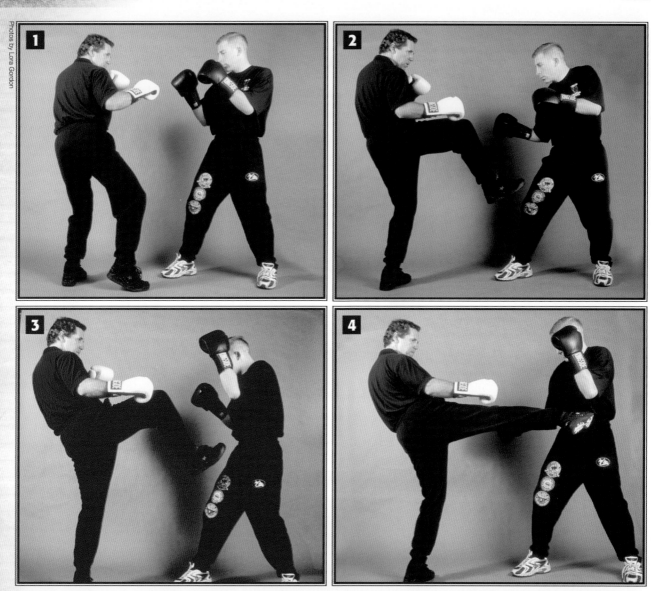

Photos by Lara Gordon

In traditional *jeet kune do* instruction, a progressive indirect attack is typically recognized in the use of a fake attack. In *Jun Fan* kickboxing, a progressive indirect attack does not incorporate a fake but relies on a change in speed, timing or distance. In this sequence, the author (left) delivers a slow front kick (1-3), then changes the speed and timing as he converts it to an angling round kick (4).

poll, has for years taught the importance of technique execution.

A personal student of Lee's, Lewis learned the five ways of attack in the manner defined in this article. He claims his experience has taught him that fighters should understand that their opponent can be categorized as a blocker (one who attempts to block an attack), a jammer (one who typically tries to rush toward an attack) or a runner (one who attempts to evade or retreat from an attack).

Although this information typically is not presented in JKD circles, it represents the necessary defensive pattern required for fully understanding the nature of offensively approaching an opponent contained in Lee's five ways of attack.

Against a blocker or a jammer, fighters who prefer not to give ground should employ the progressive indirect attack, hand immobilization attack and single direct attack. Attack by drawing is used against a blocker only when you incorporate a faking technique. As the blocker attempts to intercept the faked attack, he becomes vulnerable to the completed technique.

Jerry Beasley (right) initiates a progressive indirect attack lead-hand punch by changing from head level (1-2) to solar-plexus level (3), then follows up with a single direct attack to the face (4). In *Jun Fan* kickboxing, attack by combination involves using any two ways of attack—in this case, a progressive indirect attack and a single direct attack.

It's All Good

Some martial artists prefer to argue over the historical significance of a limited assortment of techniques, while others are not satisfied with the techniques passed on by Lee and therefore are forever engaged in the discovery of new arts and ways. However, it would seem that a more thorough understanding of the five ways of attack should result in a feeling of satisfaction that Lee had, in fact, developed a total program. Instead, JKD is unfortunately divided between the historically correct, anti-change group and the new-art conceptual group. Is one side right and the other wrong?

In view of the fact that Lee died before he completed his art or wrote down any concrete guidelines for it, we must make our own conclusions as to which interpretations are valid. We know that JKD must reflect greatly the methods and techniques taught by Lee from 1967 to 1973. However, the variation that exists in the interpretations of events and skills confined to those years leads this researcher to doubt that there will ever be harmony in the JKD world.

Jun Fan kickboxing attempts to accurately bridge the historically correct and modern conceptual interpretations with the fighting strategies of Lee and Lewis. Still, the reader must be cautioned that it should not be considered the only way to absorb JKD. However, as the kickboxing method emerges, it will no doubt represent a viable third approach to solving the riddle of JKD.

Perhaps that's what Lee would have wanted: to challenge us to make our own decisions by trial and error and to avoid at all cost the blind following of tradition—even if that tradition is a product of the search for jeet kune do.

截 拳 道

Jeet Kune Do Grappling, Part 1: When to Do It and When to Not Even Think About It

by William Holland — April 2003

Most people familiar with Bruce Lee have heard volumes spoken about his superhuman speed, amazing agility and spectacular street-fighting savvy. However, they are almost always surprised to discover that Lee invested a considerable amount of time in learning the grappling arts. If you need proof, flip to the Tools chapter of *Tao of Jeet Kune Do*, and you'll notice numerous sketches of the "Little Dragon's" favorite throwing, choking and joint-locking moves. He knew that no matter how much a person might want to stay in punching or kicking range, a real fight can go to the pavement in a heartbeat. That's why grappling has always been part of the arsenal of a complete *jeet kune do* fighter.

Before Royce Gracie debuted in the Ultimate Fighting Championship, most skilled practitioners of pugilism—those who weren't into JKD—spent their time mastering hand and foot strikes. The fighters with a little more gumption spiced up their workouts with a dash of elbows and knees. Although many practiced judo and wrestling, they were just "grappling" and not really "fighting." But that was then and this is now. The rules have changed, and smart fighters in and out of the octagon have taken up cross-training in the striking and grappling arts. JKD practitioners and a few other nonconformists have always done it, but it's still a great time to re-examine Bruce Lee's take on ground combat.

Ground Rules

Unlike judo, sport *jujutsu* and wrestling, JKD is meant for only one thing: the type of fighting that occurs on streets and in back alleys. As such, certain principles are emphasized when a JKD practitioner employs grappling in his overall blend of tactics and tools.

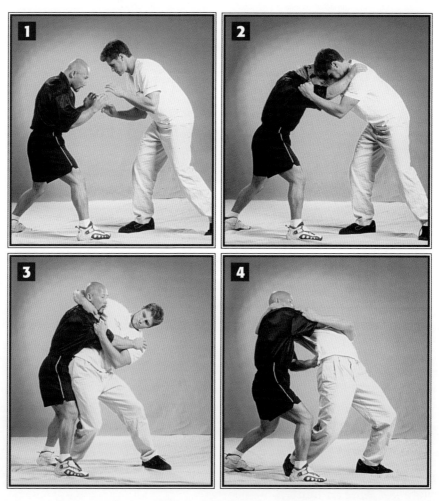

In *jeet kune do*, learning how to fight in all ranges means learning how to grapple as well as how to defend against grappling. William Holland (left) squares off with his opponent (1). The two men close the distance and tie up (2). The opponent positions his hips under Holland's center of gravity in preparation for a throw (3), but Holland counters the technique by shifting his body backward, pushing with his left arm and pulling with his right (4). With his balance ruined, the opponent has no choice but to fall backward.

The *jeet kune do* fighter tries to be ready for anything during a fight. Here, William Holland (right) faces off against a grappler (1) and enters into a clinch (2). He then grabs the opponent's lead leg—or traps it if he tries to kick (3). Next, the JKD stylist executes a leg-sweep takedown, leaving the other man horizontal (4). Holland wraps his left arm around the trapped ankle for an Achilles lock, and to keep the assailant from squirming, he uses his right foot to pin his left thigh to the ground (5). The entire time, the JKD practitioner remains mobile and able to punch and kick.

For one, the JKD fighter trains to be proficient in all ranges of combat: kicking, punching, infighting (also called trapping) and grappling. Being balanced in all four and trying to eliminate any weak links are the keys to becoming a skilled martial artist. Therefore, a JKD stylist can use grappling when he closes the distance, when the opponent closes the distance, when the opponent counters, after the opponent grabs his kick and so on. It's part of the flow.

Another key element of JKD is the need to maintain options while grappling. Although the student may be entangled in a ground position, he strives to maintain his ability to score a decisive punch, head butt, knee thrust or elbow smash while eliminating those attacks from the opponent's option list.

Although grappling may happen by design or default, the JKD stylist tries to maintain a superior position and the option of rising to his feet at anytime to get mobile and strike back. Because he is always focused on reality in combat, he may opt to use grappling in one situation while avoiding it in another. He knows Sun Tzu's words of wisdom: The intelligent fighter brings his opponent to the field of battle and is not brought there by him. He takes his adversary to the ground when it suits his needs and avoids going to the ground when it might put him at risk. The following are some of the guidelines he strives to follow.

When Not to Grapple

Even though the JKD practitioner may not want to grapple in a given scenario, his opponent can take away his choice. Therefore, he learns how to take the war to the ground and trains until he can hold his own there. But if given a choice, he will resist becoming locked in a clinch or tumbling to the ground in certain situations:

- **Against an Opponent With a Blade:** Most instructors advise against closing the distance on or clinching with a knife-wielding enemy. Until the JKD fighter takes away or controls the weapon, he has no business getting in close. Of course, if the knifer charges in and leaves the defender no alternative, he will not hesitate to disarm or immobilize him, then throw him head over heels. In most other situations, however, the rule is maintain distance and mobility, and seize any opportunity to blind him, break his kneecap or damage his weapon hand.

 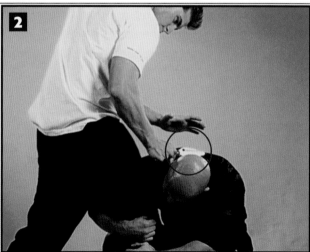

Jeet kune do instructors implore their students to never grapple against a knife. It's hazardous when you clinch (1) and when you shoot in for a takedown (2).

- **Against Multiple Opponents:** Whenever more than one attacker is present or possible, the ground is the last place the JKD practitioner wants to be. Even if he attains the much-vaunted mount position, he cannot protect himself from a swift kick in the ribs or knife in the kidney. The immediacy of this guideline was driven home for me when a friend who trains in Brazilian *jiu-jitsu* and works as a police officer got in a fight while relaxing in a bar off-duty. His first instinct was to take the assailant to the floor, and he did. While he was jockeying for position to finish a lock, another hoodlum approached and kicked him numerous times in the back and head—all while the cop's backup gun was visible on his ankle.

Jeet kune do practitioners try to avoid locking up with multiple opponents because it is virtually impossible to control and finish more than one person at a time.

- **When Mobility or Escape Is Essential:** If a situation has the potential to get ugly, the JKD student knows that a hasty exit is often the best response. Remember the Los Angeles riots and the more recent "celebrations" in which Lakers fans went wild after the team won? Fires were started, cars were trashed, stores were looted, and people were dragged from their vehicles and robbed. Obviously, these are battles best fought by others, but if a martial artist is forced to defend life and limb, he needs to stay on his feet and be able to retreat. Sometimes the smartest battles are the ones not fought.

- **Against a Superior Grappler:** If a JKD practitioner has a bigger, stronger, fiercer person in his face and that guy happens to be a more skilled ground fighter, he will attempt to force the assailant to fight a different game. The JKD stylist always strives to become skilled in kicking, punching, trapping and grappling ranges so that if grappling is not the key to victory on a given day, he can switch to another range—hopefully one in which he has the advantage over his opponent.

- **On a High-Risk Surface:** It doesn't take too much imagination to conceive of situations in which going to the ground can be hazardous to one's health. How about a construction site where nails, tools or sharp objects are lying about, or a back alley where broken bottles, used syringes and discarded

The preferred *jeet kune do* method for confronting multiple assailants involves rapid strikes and mobility. William Holland (right) faces two opponents (1). As the larger one punches, Holland angles slightly to his left to avoid the strike (2). The JKD stylist then plows a low stop-kick into the other man's lead knee using the "closest weapon, closest target" concept (3). He immediately yanks on the same man's neck to destroy his balance and prepares to maneuver around him (4). Next, Holland scoots behind the injured person and uses his body as a shield (5). Finally, he shoves the smaller assailant into the larger one to create enough distance and time to escape (6).

auto parts litter the pavement? When a JKD practitioner stays on his feet, he improves his chances of avoiding all those nasty things.

When to Grapple

In addition to learning when not to grapple, the JKD student learns when going to the ground is the preferred course of action:

- **When Apprehending an Unarmed Assailant:** If the odds—relative skill, size, speed, mobility and so on—are stacked in his favor and the opponent has no weapon or cohorts, the humane thing for the JKD stylist to do is take his opponent down and control him. That diminishes the need to shoot, stab or beat him into submission. From day one, police officers learn this strategy, which is covered in their use-of-force doctrine. They are taught to go from verbal commands to control techniques to pain-threshold moves to nonlethal weapons before resorting to deadly force or firearms. In instances when they have a less-than-cooperative person they must arrest, detain or otherwise control, grappling can help them accomplish the task and keep them out of court.

- **Against an Inferior Grappler:** When the JKD practitioner does not have to worry about bladed weapons, multiple assailants or dangerous ground, he can opt to shoot in, take down his opponent and maneuver

him into his favorite submission hold. That approach is particularly valuable when he is confronted by a skilled striker because—whether you wish to admit it or not—a good grappler can outmaneuver and hogtie most stand-up fighters in a flash. And while most smart martial artists have figured out that a complete self-defense arsenal includes takedowns and grappling skills, many of them have yet to spend much time on the mat.

- **When Injuries Must Be Avoided:** This situation gets back to the humanitarian angle. The JKD fighter is taught to forget about the blood and guts of Hollywood movies and think about the litigious nature of American

The Four Options

The *jeet kune do* practitioner has four main options in any grappling encounter. Using his sensitivity, he can flow from one to another and back again to suit his needs and the reactions of his adversary. Those options are the following:

- cutting off the flow of blood to the brain
- cutting off the flow of oxygen to the lungs
- inflicting pain
- exerting control and manipulation

Depending on the skill and physical attributes of the opponent, he can go in with a purpose and inflict his will, or he can use his tactical awareness to take the path of least resistance. If the blood supply is available, constrict it. If the windpipe is open, snatch it. If a joint or pressure point is begging to be assaulted, do it. And when in doubt, hit. —*W.H.*

society. When Uncle Charlie has had one too many spiked punches at cousin Susie's wedding, the JKD stylist is better off taking a firm hold on his arm and escorting him to a more peaceful place.

- **When There Is No Alternative:** In the ring, in a back alley and in life, there are certain things that the martial artist has control over and other things that he doesn't. But no matter what happens, he always has control over how he deals with them. He may not be given a choice about whether to grapple, but he must deal with it. Once he acknowledges that combat on the ground is a possibility, he can train to prevail there.

The JKD Way

Jeet kune do grappling follows the same approach as JKD fighting in other ranges. It should be kept simple, direct and effective. The practitioner should strive for totality and a full utilization of his skills and strengths while minimizing his weaknesses. As opposed to memorizing dozens of techniques or forms, the JKD stylist who switches to grappling mode is more apt to focus on the feel and flow of his opponent and how his body, joints and limbs are positioned.

Remember that the JKD fighter is a finely tuned punching and kicking machine and will almost always strive to maintain a striking capacity—even when he's horizontal. The energy drills and sensitivity he has gained from sticky-hand drills and trapping exercises work well on the ground, and they can give him a sense of position, flow and opportunity that others seldom enjoy.

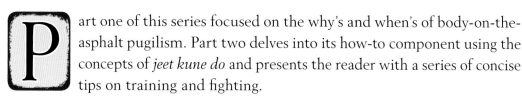

Jeet Kune Do Grappling, Part 2: Offensive Tactics for the Ground

by William Holland — May 2003

Part one of this series focused on the why's and when's of body-on-the-asphalt pugilism. Part two delves into its how-to component using the concepts of *jeet kune do* and presents the reader with a series of concise tips on training and fighting.

- A jeet kune do fighter strives to be proficient at all ranges of combat in all scenarios. He knows that against an aggressive fighter, he may need to use an intercepting fist, a stop-kick or a grappling technique.

- A grappling exchange can begin after the JKD stylist takes his opponent down, after he is taken down by his opponent or after one or both parties fall.

- One of the best ways for the JKD fighter to grapple with his adversary is to first convince him that grappling is the last thing on his agenda. If he wants to shoot in for a single- or double-leg takedown, he should fake a jab or cross to his opponent's head. As the opponent defends high, he will probably leave his legs unprotected. Likewise, if the JKD practitioner wants to clinch, he can fake a low-line punch or takedown to encourage his opponent to expose his upper body.

Voice of Experience

In the 22-plus years he has worked as a bodyguard and private investigator, William Holland has protected the well-being of thousands of people— in the middle of the Los Angeles riots, in the heat of domestic violence and on the drug-infested streets of Southern California.

"I have had more than my share of reality and truth in combat," he says. "Unfortunately, I have been shot and stabbed, and been the recipient of more than two dozen death threats in my career. So far, I am still in one piece."

It is that background that he drew from to write the two-part feature on *jeet kune do* grappling. —*Editors*

- The key to being nontelegraphic lies in maintaining a poker face and a poker body. The JKD stylist does not reveal his intentions until he is ready to force his adversary to commit to a defense.
- When closing the gap for a clinch or takedown, the JKD practitioner pays attention to his opponent's perimeter. A boxer may allow him to get closer because he is used to fighting up close. A kicker may lash out from farther away because he is used to keeping distance between himself and his opponent. In either case, awareness is essential.
- To move into punching range without taking a boot to the belly, the JKD stylist is prepared to enter with a real or fake kick. Once in punching range, he may use a rapid combination to force his foe to cover up, thus opening a clear path to his legs.
- Another JKD ploy for closing the gap and getting into punching range involves trapping the opponent's lead arm before advancing.
- Against an aggressive opponent, the JKD fighter may prefer to use counterfighting. He will wait for his opponent to step forward with a jab or recover after a kick, then switch into slam-down mode.
- Once the JKD practitioner gets into tie-up range, he may not need to go to the ground. His striking and infighting skills can enable him to use punches, elbow strikes, kicks, knee thrusts and head butts while minimizing the other man's ability to resist.
- The JKD fighter uses the concept of circumstantial spontaneity: Once he analyzes his opponent's physical ability, skill level and fighting style, he employs the way of attack that most efficiently overcomes the other man's defenses. Those ways of attack are outlined below.

Simple Direct Attack

- With respect to striking mode, Bruce Lee used to say, "When in doubt, hit." The same holds true for the type of close-range fighting that takes place in a clinch.
- If the JKD stylist has the advantage of size and power and is skilled at grappling, he may want to go directly for a takedown or submission hold.

NOT-SO-SIMPLE DIRECT ATTACK: William Holland (right) assumes a fighting stance in front of a striker (1). Because Holland believes he has a grappling advantage, he launches a backhand strike (2) and a left cross (3), both of which the opponent nullifies. Holland then moves on to his true mission: to lock the opponent's lead arm (4) and force him to the ground (5). Once he falls, the *jeet kune do* practitioner ups the pressure he exerts on the trapped limb as he uses his knee to pin the other man's head to the floor (6).

Make It Yours

It would be safe to say that most practitioners of *jeet kune do* and those martial artists who have delved into the wealth of insight provided by Bruce Lee's *Tao of Jeet Kune Do* have envisioned the ways of attack primarily from a striking perspective. I confess to having been guilty of the same offense.

For 24 years, the primary focus of my JKD training was on honing my punching and kicking skills. Although I had wrestled in high school and college, ground fighting stayed for the most part on the back burner in terms of time and effort invested.

Then along came Royce Gracie and the Ultimate Fighting Championship. Now I, like many martial artists around the world, can say I have spent the past several years mentally and physically dissecting the moves of Brazilian *jiu-jitsu* and other ground-based systems to complement the strengths of Bruce Lee's progressive art. It has allowed me to develop "my own JKD," and it can do the same for you. —W.H.

There will be little his opponent can do about it if he dives right in for a double-leg takedown and dumps his foe on his head, or if he climbs right into the mount and puts him out with an eye-popping stranglehold.

Simple Indirect Attack

- If the opponent is more skilled and less vulnerable, the JKD fighter will often progress to the indirect attack, which relies on feints for effectiveness.
- If he intends to shoot in with a single- or double-leg takedown, the JKD practitioner will set up his opponent as though he is planning to clinch or attack high. As soon as the opponent raises his guard, the JKD stylist will shoot for his legs.
- If the JKD stylist wants to clinch from the side, he will fake in the opposite direction. When the other man takes the bait and leans or moves in the desired direction, the JKD fighter will push him in the direction he just faked, then shoot in.
- On the ground, subtle movements and indications of movement can produce predictable reactions from an opponent who is susceptible to such tactics. The JKD stylist may aim a punch or palm strike at his face, and when the opponent reaches up to block or control the hand, the JKD stylist will seize the arm and lock it. If he wants to attack the neck, the martial artist will apply pressure to the eye socket or temple with his wrist bone or knuckle.

Attack by Combination

- The JKD practitioner who possesses good speed, power and endurance can use the principle of attack by combination as easily on the ground as he does on his feet.
- If the attacker tries to use a direct, penetrating move, the JKD student can counter it and, once the opportunity has passed, alter his orientation to strike a more accessible target. He executes a

SIMPLE INDIRECT ATTACK: William Holland (left) squares off with an opponent (1). He executes a lead-hand eye jab to make the opponent shift his attention to his upper-body targets (2), then shoots in and seizes his leg (3). Holland immediately wraps his right leg around the other man's calf and pushes against his thigh (4) to force him to the ground (5). Once there, Holland can finish him with strikes or a lock.

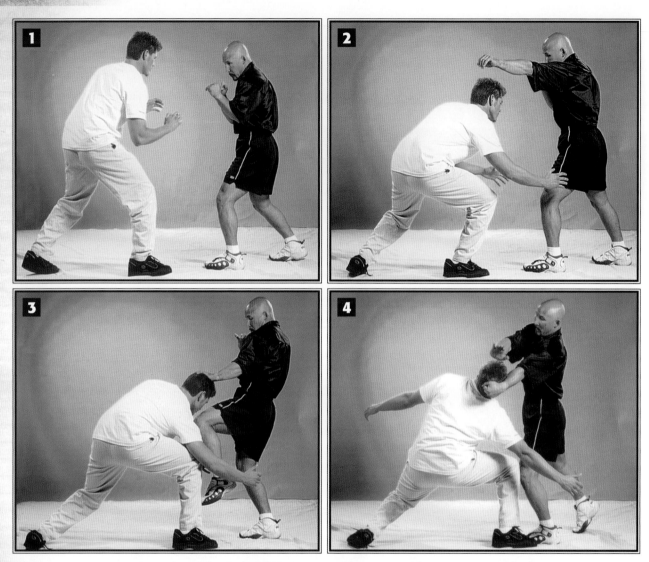

ATTACK BY DRAWING: The grappler (left) prepares to attack William Holland (1). Holland initiates a lead-hand jab to make the opponent think he has left his legs unprotected. The opponent ducks to avoid the punch, then shoots in for the expected takedown (2). The *jeet kune do* expert immediately raises his knee and smashes it into the other man's face (3). He then grabs his hair and issues a palm-heel strike to the nose (4).

rapid succession of moves with speed, intensity and ferocity, overwhelming his opponent and forcing him into defensive mode until he can gain an arm lock, choke or as Lee used to say, anything that scores.

- While executing an attack sequence, the JKD stylist maintains his balance and readiness to negate a counter from his opponent.

Attack by Drawing

- During stand-up fighting, the JKD practitioner uses attack by drawing

IMMOBILIZATION ATTACK: William Holland (left) and his opponent face each other (1). Holland enters with a low-line jab, which the opponent blocks (2). The *jeet kune do* stylist follows up with a maiming technique aimed at the radial nerve on the forearm (3). While the opponent is still numb from the strike, Holland executes a left cross to the head (4) and a Thai kick to the leg (5). With his adversary stunned and off-balance, Holland takes his back and transitions to a choke (6).

to lure his opponent in and counterattack or intercept him while he is launching his own assault. That works because most people tend to forget about their own defensive vulnerability when they smell blood.

- During a ground fight, the JKD practitioner can use attack by drawing just as productively. In a closely matched contest, he can gain the advantage by baiting his opponent into going for an arm or for position. When he does the expected, the JKD fighter exploits the opening that results when he inevitably extends himself or leaves a body part unprotected.

- When baiting his opponent, the JKD stylist needs a keen sense of timing, positioning and accuracy if he is to cut off the other man and sink in his own hook. Counterfighting is known as the art of masters and champions, and it is indeed a skill that takes much training and tactical knowledge. If it is used weakly or halfheartedly, it will leave the martial artist open to attack.

Immobilization Attack

- The JKD student knows that trapping or otherwise immobilizing his opponent's defensive tools can open an avenue to strike. He also knows that the immobilization attack is a highly developed skill that few people master.

- When the JKD fighter attempts to secure a position, lock or hold, his opponent will often defend himself by placing his hand or arm in the way. The action does not surprise the experienced practitioner.

- If the opponent uses his arm to obstruct the JKD stylist's movement, the JKD stylist simply takes it out of play. He may use his body as a barrier to keep the hand from reaching its goal. If his body cannot be used, he may employ his arm to restrict the movement of his opponent's arm. That gives him a greater chance of securing a firm hold or strategic position, and it carries him one step closer to victory.

截 拳 道

Jeet Kune Do Ground Game:
4 Supplemental Disciplines That Will
Improve Your Ability to Fight on the Mat!

by Paul Vunak — August 2003

After Bruce Lee died in 1973, Dan Inosanto became responsible for keeping *jeet kune do* alive. He soul-searched for a few years, then opened the Filipino Kali Academy as a laboratory in which every JKD principle, concept and philosophy—as well as those from outside sources that were candidates for inclusion in the system—could be dissected and tested. What made the school so good was that anyone could come in and challenge us. All a person had to do was put on the gloves, and within moments, it was obvious whose truth was more functional.

That search for truth made us fall in love with Brazilian *jiu-jitsu* in the mid-1980s. Various members of the Gracie family had set up shop in Southern California, and local martial artists were beginning to talk. We heard about their challenge matches and noted how their philosophy and ours were nearly identical. The only major difference was we did it on our feet, while they did it on the ground.

Shortly thereafter, Brazilian grappling started seeping into the JKD matrix. That's not to say Lee's art lacked ground functionality; Larry Hartsell had proved

Photo by Rick Hustead

Bruce Lee was 50 years ahead of his time, says Diego Sanchez, MMA veteran, in a *Black Belt* interview.

time and again that JKD worked in any situation. However, none of us had ever experienced the moves and transitions the Gracies were doing.

The more Brazilian jiu-jitsu I learned, the less I knew. Every time I believed I had reached a certain level, some 60-year-old Brazilian would come in and mop the floor with me. (Imagine what it's like having some old man wrap his arms around your neck and whisper, "This is what it feels like to die, boy!"—and then waking up to those same ruthless eyes.) Experiences like those taught me to appreciate the JKD paradigm: When someone is better than you, find a way to cheat. That awakening led to the genesis of the JKD ground game.

Lee's prime directive of "using no way as way" gave us the freedom to look at any art that might give us an advantage—help us cheat, so to speak—on the mat. Different practitioners adopted different disciplines according to their personal preferences. Because space does not permit me to discuss them all, I will limit myself to three that mesh with Brazilian jiu-jitsu and fit in with the way of jeet kune do.

Sambo for Leg Attacks

The cornerstone of Brazilian jiu-jitsu is its repertoire of techniques designed for fighting while you're on your back. That differentiates the Brazilian ground methodology from the American ground methodology, for in many styles of wrestling, once your shoulders are pinned to the mat, the match is over.

The Brazilians, however, mastered a position they call the guard: It involves lying on your back, placing your opponent between your legs and wrapping your legs around his torso. From that position, you can defend yourself quite well—and attack with sweeps, throws, chokes and locks.

The traditional way to escape is called "passing the guard." You remove yourself from between your opponent's legs and reposition your body across his torso. If you are not proficient at passing the guard, you will be stuck between your opponent's legs forever—or until he catches you in an arm lock, a sweep or a triangle choke.

One secret to beating the Brazilian jiu-jitsu guard was born behind the Iron Curtain. The art, called *sambo*, is not technically dissimilar from judo and jiu-jitsu, but it does possess a unique emphasis. While judo focuses on flips and throws and jiu-jitsu relies on establishing a base and effecting a tight transition into a finishing hold, sambo emphasizes locking the ankles, knees and hips.

Picture yourself entwined in a Brazilian jiu-jitsu black belt's guard. Your task is to pass it, and to accomplish that, you must beat him at a game he's been playing four hours a day since he was in grade school. What do you do? If you lack the skills needed to pass his guard using Brazilian jiu-jitsu, your best bet may be to attack one of his legs using sambo.

Of course, Brazilian jiu-jitsu teaches foot and leg locks, but because the art doesn't emphasize them, they are not second nature for most practitioners. It may take you years to perfect your ability to pass the guard using jiu-jitsu, but it takes only a few months to learn how to lock a foot, and that can bring victory.

MMA instructor Gokor Chivichyan is also a well-known *sambo* champion.

Yoga for Breath Control

To see how yoga fits into the JKD ground game, you must understand two truths: First, breathing is the cornerstone of yoga, and second, without proper breathing, ground fighting is a lost cause.

Yoga teaches you to inhale through your nose, bypassing your chest and going straight to your lower abdomen. Watching a practitioner of the Indian art breathe is amazing. It does not appear that his lungs are inflating his chest. All you see is his stomach moving in and out.

If you observe a novice grappler rolling around on the mat, two things become evident: He holds his breath, and he hyperventilates. Those faults are the nemesis of all ground fighters. Interestingly, they cause a similar physiological response: insufficient oxygen in the brain. When that occurs, endurance plunges. It is not uncommon to see two well-conditioned athletes from other sports grapple for five minutes and almost faint from exhaustion.

When you practice yoga, your breathing becomes slow, soft and steady. It is no longer a series of short, rapid breaths. The unmistakable sound is similar to what you hear in a theater when someone is talking: shooooosh.

When I started training with the Gracies, I would hear

Former UFC champ Frank Shamrock harnesses the power of yoga in no-holds-barred training.

that incessant noise for hours every day. A year later, I asked Rickson Gracie about its relevance. "It took you one year to ask the most important question in jiu-jitsu, my friend," he replied. "As long as we hear that noise, we automatically know two things: We're not holding our breath, and we're not panting like a dog."

Plyometrics to Build Your Body

Plyometrics is a term used to describe a group of exercises that has its roots in Europe, where it was first called "jump training." It is designed to link strength with speed of movement to produce power. All professional athletes use plyometrics for a simple reason: It enables the muscles to reach maximum strength in minimal time.

Plyometrics can dramatically increase your explosiveness, which is a primary attribute of the best grapplers. A hip throw, an armbar and an elbow escape have explosive elements in them. Explosive power enables you to create space with short bursts of movement. If you're

Striving for the Goal

Despite the rise and fall of numerous martial arts fads, interest in *jeet kune do,* the fighting philosophy Bruce Lee and Dan Inosanto created and refined, never wanes. The pair spent years investigating every style they could find, then analyzed each one to separate the concepts that were salient to street combat. The results were integrated into the ever-changing JKD matrix. Whenever they came upon a new art or technique, they did not hesitate to alter or tweak it to fit their paradigm. What exactly was their paradigm? The street—where anything goes and where there are no rules. —*P.V.*

Photos by Sara Fogan

Plyometrics can help martial artists increase their explosiveness. Here, Paul Vunak demonstrates an energy-intensive sequence that could be used in the no-holds-barred ring or on the street. As soon as his opponent clinches, Vunak positions his hands for an escape attempt (1). He then lifts the other man's elbows and scoots under his right arm (2-3). Once he has the opponent's back (4), he lifts him (5) and slams him to the mat (6).

Trash Day

Most martial arts instructors would have you believe that street fights unfold within the parameters of their style, their way. *Taekwondo* people tell you that every fight has a litany of high kicks. Boxers insist that every violent encounter is based on the jab, hook, cross, uppercut and overhand. *Aikido* people argue that a street brawl is a series of joint locks.

All that leads to the cornerstone of Bruce Lee's passion: convincing the public that there is "no way." In fact, one of his most frequently repeated expressions was "using no way as way." The implementation of that philosophy gave him and Dan Inosanto the impunity to do whatever works. They examined the myriad of techniques of the martial arts, found out which ones did not work and threw them away. What they kept is the art we call *jeet kune do. —P.V.*

on the bottom, it can help you keep your opponent off-balance. If you're on top, it can make your ground and pound more effective, especially if you add head butts, knees and elbows.

Isometric strength is the ability to exert force in a fixed position—when the length of the muscle and the angle of the joint do not change. It is important because as a grappler, you may have to hold your opponent in a vicelike guard or grip his collar for minutes on end.

All martial arts movements, especially grappling techniques, require stout abdominal muscles and a strong "speed center." That term refers to the group of muscles that initiate, assist and stabilize all your movements. They include the abs, lower back, hip flexors and extensors, hip rotators and glutes.

Good core stability gives you strength during an unstable movement, and that's essential on the ground. An athlete may be able to bench-press 300 pounds, but that has nothing to do with grappling because you don't have the luxury of lying on a flat surface with a balanced weight above you. Instead, you must fight from wherever you fall. One shoulder might be pinned against the floor, while the other is free. Core-stability exercises teach your body to move as a unit under such conditions, in essence strengthening the weakest links.

Kino Mutai for Shock and Awe

Kino mutai is the Philippine art of biting and pinching. JKD practitioners refer to it as biting and eye gouging because their preferred area to pinch is the eyeball.

Its roots lie partially in the fact that many Filipino *escrimadors* possess an attribute that's rare in the West: incredible grip strength. It's a byproduct of wielding heavy sticks, swords and knives all day long. When that hand power is combined with biting, it becomes another way of cheating on the ground.

Kino mutai shines when you're stuck in the bottom position under a large man with a good base. If you follow the rules, it could take you as long as 10 minutes to work your way out, and that's fine if you're in a match. However, if you're rolling around on the asphalt, 10 minutes is an eternity. That's the perfect time to use

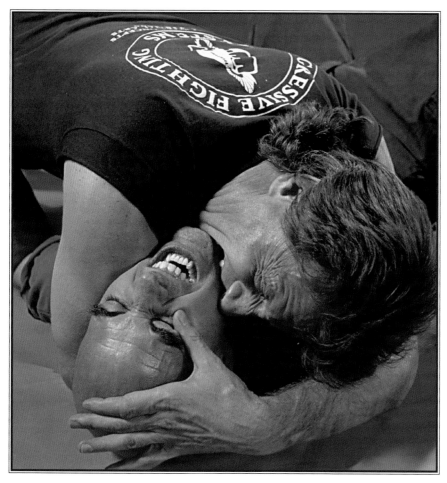

Kino mutai is the Philippine art of biting and eye gouging. With the proper *jujutsu* hold to keep your opponent from squirming, you can use both skills at the same time.

a bite or eye gouge to create enough space to scramble to your knees and escape.

Now, you may be thinking anyone can bite. That's true, but the difference between nipping someone and employing kino mutai is vast. The art involves knowing how to do it, where to do it and when to do it. When a kino mutai practitioner takes action, he does it as an uninterrupted bite. That means he knows the exact places on your body to target. He'll grab hold of you with his iron grip and attack areas that you cannot easily reach. It might take you minutes to pull him off.

Gnawing on an opponent may sound brutal, and in this day and age, it can be hazardous to your health to come into contact with another person's blood, but consider the alternative. While not every fight is to the death, it's comforting to have an ultimate weapon in your arsenal.

Conclusion

JKD cultivates your ability to solve problems. When you're on the ground, your first problem is often how to escape from your opponent's guard. Sambo provides a solution. A second problem is how to take in enough oxygen, and for that you have yoga. A third problem is how to escape from being pinned down—which is when kino mutai can save your skin.

Remember that the aforementioned arts are simply pieces of the puzzle that make up my JKD ground matrix. Your matrix may be slightly different. As Bruce Lee implored us all to do, "Absorb what is useful, reject what is useless, and add what is specifically your own."

截 拳 道

Bruce Lee's First Generation:
James DeMile Sets the Record Straight
Regarding the Early Years of Jeet Kune Do

Interview by Paul J. Bax — February 2004

B ruce Lee lived in Seattle from 1959 to 1964, and during that time, he collected an inner circle of students who would become known as the first generation. James DeMile was one of those early disciples, having started training with Lee in 1959 and continued until 1962. In numerous interviews, the former Air Force heavyweight boxing champion has covered topics that ranged from how he and Lee met to how they trained. In this *Black Belt* exclusive, DeMile, who later founded the art of *wing chun do*, revisits some of those issues to clarify questions that have been on the minds of martial artists and Bruce Lee aficionados for decades.

Q: Recently, the Jun Fan Jeet Kune Do Nucleus dissolved. Years before that, the same fate befell the JKD Society. Is it a lost cause for Bruce Lee students like yourself to try to organize an association to disseminate his teachings?

Years after his training with Bruce Lee had ended, James DeMile founded the art of *wing chun do*.

Photo courtesy of James DeMile

Bruce Lee snapped this photo of (left to right) students Ed Hart, Leroy Garcia, James DeMile and Jesse Glover in 1962.

James DeMile: Yes. There is not one voice but many; yet none of them knows what Bruce really meant in his thoughts and teachings.

Q: It seems as if all his students claim to have learned the best of his theories and techniques, but you have said he never taught anyone how to beat him. Please explain.

DeMile: It's a very important statement and easily understood by anyone who wanted to be the best, developed a way to achieve it and then realized that if you show it to someone, they would improve on it and beat you. The reason I broke away from Bruce's classes in Jun Fan was that he left out pieces of the puzzle that made everything work. He de-emphasized the centerline, closed *bi jong* (ready stance) and spring energy. He continued this way of teaching in *jeet kune do*. Bruce could make Jun Fan and JKD work because he had the basics. In all the years I have known people who trained in anything Bruce taught in his later periods, I have never known them to use the basic concepts as Bruce applied them.

Q: You once said, "Bruce never taught the applied concept of the surge punch because he felt to do so would invite someone to beat him."

DeMile: [That brings up] the two-seconds-or-less concept. Bruce knew that if you had a single punch that would bring down anyone, it could be used against him. The punch seems to be more exposed [these days], yet I find the application is still missing. Being able to hit hard and being able to hit your target are two different things.

Q: Lee reportedly told you: "If a person learns my punching and closing techniques, that's all he needs to know. With the element of surprise, you can just leap in like a bolt of lightning and blow anyone away regardless of his rank or style." In today's world of grappling-related arts, do you believe Lee could still make his punches work that well?

DeMile: Without a doubt. You must remember that most grapplers are willing to leap in and take a punch in order to take the opponent down. In most cases, this can work. Bruce was like a shadow that always seemed to disappear, no matter how fast you attacked. He would hit you at angles. He could dislocate your jaw, crush your temple, crack your clavicle or split a muscle—all in less than a blink. While you were rushing [in] all protected, he would redirect your energy and spring-load your awkward position, then fire at any number of targets.

Q: You said you once engaged in a conversation with Dan Inosanto about several tournament champions who had sparred with Lee and failed to score. Can you expound on that?

DeMile: It is hard to recall the exact conversation that took place many years ago, but this is the gist of it. Danny had seen Bruce spar with [them] and said he neutralized everything they tried. Lee's ability to close, trap and shut down any attack was amazing. I did not doubt this since I had had personal experience with his skills. Bruce was a street fighter, and they were tournament players. There is a definite difference between the two. I have always been more than happy to explain the differences to those who think that winning trophies and smashing heads are the same thing.

Q: In another interview, you said Lee could have beaten anyone regardless of size and strength. With martial artists now reaching new levels in their training, would Lee have enjoyed the same superiority over them as he did when you knew him?

Photo courtesy of Paul J. Bax

Jesse Glover (left) and author Paul J. Bax (center) pose with James DeMile at the first meeting of the Jun Fan Jeet Kune Do Nucleus.

DeMile: Yes. The reason is what he did and how he did it. Today's fighter is bigger and stronger yet does much of the same thing when fighting. It is difficult to explain but easy when doing it in person. A large part of the problem in communicating Bruce's skills is that most people do not understand what a street fight is. It is not a tournament, not the Ultimate Fighting Championship, K-1 or the Sabaki Challenge. It is Neanderthal. The only goal is to hurt or kill the opponent. It is stupid and mindless, yet it happens everyday. Bruce had two levels of action: two seconds or less and play. That meant the fight was over in a blink, or he played cat-and-mouse because he had no respect for the person's skills. I do not care how strong you are, what rank you are or what style you are; if you cannot see it coming, you cannot stop it. If, at the other end of that invisible movement was the floating punch, then it was over before it began.

Q: A *wing chun* kung fu instructor named Robert Yeung provided you with insight into the Chinese art. Did he also help you understand the way Lee practiced it?

DeMile: Robert Yeung was a wing chun purist. He lived it and breathed it. He was the first one in line to defend the honor of wing chun. He came to visit me where I was teaching in Honolulu, to find out who this guy was that said he was teaching wing chun. He really came to challenge me. He watched my class and approached me afterward to ask what I was teaching. I said, "Wing chun." Without a smile, he said, "No, you're not. You are using the terms of wing chun but not doing the techniques correctly."

Photo courtesy of James DeMile

Bruce Lee and James DeMile met in this parking lot during the late 1950s and early '60s for their workouts.

I found this an interesting statement since I had never known anyone but Bruce to practice wing chun. He told me he had trained in Yip Man's school in Hong Kong. At this point, I think Robert became aware that I meant no disrespect but was just ignorant as to what wing chun was. We sat down, and I explained my training with Bruce and his use of the term in our training. Robert explained that Bruce's wing chun training was limited since he only trained for three years. Although very skilled in general applications, he felt Bruce lacked insight into the true art.

Bruce was not really interested in wing chun; he was only interested in fighting. Robert felt this is why Bruce did things so differently. He was very focused and only gleaned the techniques and concepts that had value for him. Bruce's later teaching in America reflected this thought, since he always related to fighting when evaluating a technique or concept. He would teach a technique for a month and suddenly drop it in favor of something else. Robert felt Bruce deserved a lot of credit for his creative insight into the art of fighting. However, Robert was only interested in the art of wing chun and assumed that Bruce used wing chun as a springboard or starting point for his own discoveries.

Q: Had Lee already created an advanced fighting method while still in Seattle?

DeMile: Bruce evolved all through his short life. However, in those first few years, he discovered his personal answers to be the best fighter. Once discovered, he filed them away and began his quest to create the best martial art. His belief that a fight should not take over two seconds was basic to his discoveries. The longer the fight, the more chance for luck to come into play. Bruce wanted to control the outcome, not hope he was going to be lucky.

One of the most important concepts that Bruce shared with me was that you could become a master of a few techniques but never a lot. He felt that if you could define the elements of a fight and design techniques to directly overwhelm them, you were developing the ultimate system. If the total list of techniques did not exceed 10, becoming a master of them was very realistic. I have followed this thought, both in my teaching and my training. I am a good teacher and know my material well, but my students often become better than me in many elements of wing chun do. But for my own purposes, I know less than 10 techniques that I have total confidence will wipe out anyone I should have to fight. In my demonstrations, I try to share this concept so people will have some insight as to why Bruce was so effective in his survival skills.

Photo courtesy of James DeMile

The upper-left window of Ruby Chow's restaurant in Seattle was part of Bruce Lee's bedroom.

Q: Speaking of survival skills, didn't Lee use to train with firearms as well as with his empty hands?

DeMile: Bruce liked to fire guns. He and Leroy Garcia used to do a lot of shooting. However, I do not believe Bruce trained with guns.

Q: Could you explain Lee's "spring load" concept?

DeMile: It was a critical element of Bruce's ability to trap and control an opponent. His "spring load" was like a bad smell you could not get rid of. Once he touched you, no matter how you twisted or turned, you could not get away from him. The application was to put you into a weak position or angle and keep you there while he thumped on your head.

Q: You reportedly taught him hypnosis. How did he use the skill?

DeMile: Bruce did not like the term "hypnosis" but felt that it was a much faster way to access the subconscious than conventional meditation. Hypnosis and meditation have the same intent: to travel within and use the mental potential to accelerate training. My input was to teach him self-hypnosis and how to develop suggestions in the areas he was concerned with.

Q: There is some confusion about Lee's sharing of the one-inch punch. Many claim to have been taught it, yet you once said he taught it only to you. Are you the only person from the Seattle era to have acquired knowledge of the technique?

DeMile: I do not want to beat my own drum, but Bruce did not teach me the one-inch punch. He and I developed it. That is why I know so many details that make the punch work. In my apartment, we went over and over ways to hit at close range. Robert Yeung said wing chun had a long-range floating punch but nothing at one or two inches. Bruce knew of the wing chun punch but wanted something that would fit into his close-in trapping techniques. Since I had been a boxer, we experimented with the punching action and then explored different ways to add power. They were two separate elements. The punching action was actually the easy part; it was how to generate explosive power at an inch or less. Once we accomplished a marriage between the two, Bruce insisted I tell no one. This included Jesse [Glover] and everyone else in the early group. It was no big deal to me. Jesse spent a lot of private time with Bruce, and I am sure he knows things the rest of us don't.

I honestly forgot about the punch for many years. I never heard anything from the Jun Fan or JKD [people] regarding it. Only years later in the early '70s did I hear it mentioned. Bob Wall was on TV in Honolulu talking about being in a recent movie with Bruce. He said that Bruce showed him this punch, then demonstrated it. I was blown away. I called the station and asked Bob to stop by. He did, and I asked him to hit me. Then I told him to hit me again, only as hard as he could. It rocked me, but I did not feel the internal roll of energy that I knew was part of the punch. Bob asked me to hit him. I put a phone book to his chest and knocked him across my club and into a wall. He was stunned and said, "That was unbelievable. You should write a book on that." And that is how the *Bruce Lee's 1 and 3 Inch Power Punch* book originated. Over the years, I have run across many instructors who profess to know the punch and have never felt one that had the internal reactions of the original.

Q: A rumor holds that you and Lee had a falling out. Is there any truth to that?

DeMile: It is not a rumor; it is true. It was my fault. After I broke away from regular classes, I would go down and visit Bruce in his underground club on King Street. After one of his classes, I was talking to some of the students and they asked why I had stopped training. I mentioned that I felt Bruce was leaving out important pieces of what made things work. Bruce heard about my comments, and when I visited again, he confronted me, very uptight, and asked why I said what I did. I told him, and he said I had no right to make comments to his class. I agreed and apologized.

He [started] slapping some gloves into his palm and suggested I was challenging him. He was very upset and seemed to be pushing for a fight. I knew I was on dangerous ground. To fight Bruce when he was calm was insanity, but to do it when he was mad was to invite sudden death. The only amusing memory of the event was that in that period of my life, I carried a gun. I had it in my coat pocket, and my finger was on the trigger. I calmly thought to myself that if he leaped at me, I was going to [use it]. As it was, I apologized again, turned and walked out. That was the last time I spoke to him.

截 拳 道

Jeet Kune Do Secrets:
First-Generation Disciple
Reveals Little-Known Bruce Lee
Teachings on Self-Defense

by Jerry Poteet — July 2004

I first met Bruce Lee in 1964. At the time, I was one of Ed Parker's top *kenpo* black belts, and I had accompanied him to San Francisco to arrange the first International Karate Championship. While we were there, we decided to visit James Lee in nearby Oakland, California. His brother, Bruce, was staying with him.

James had a wooden dummy, and while we all stood around socializing, Bruce walked over and suddenly started hitting it. He exploded like a machine gun, and the power of his blows shook the house to its foundation. After everyone else backed away, I approached the dummy. Even when I put all my weight into moving it, it didn't budge. I wondered, Who is this little guy who can generate so much power? I couldn't wait to train with him.

Less than two years later, I became Bruce Lee's second student at his school in Los Angeles. He remained my teacher until he went to Hong Kong to make movies at the end of the 1960s. The fighting techniques and strategies I learned during that time were invaluable.

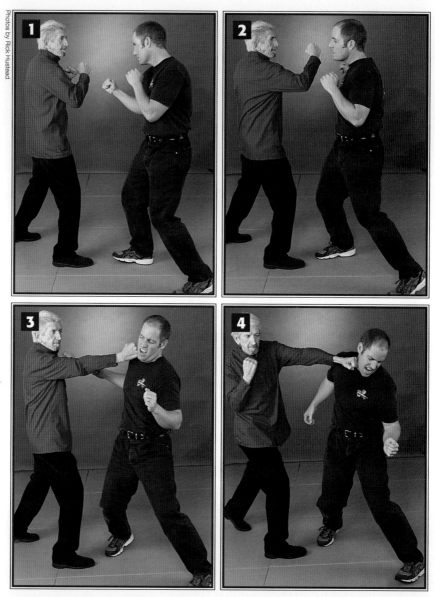

Jerry Poteet (left) faces his opponent (1). As soon as the man draws his fist back for a punch, Poteet blasts him with a backfist to the face (2-3). He immediately follows up with a cross to the chin (4).

Throw the First Punch

One day, after five of us had finished a session with Lee, he blurted out, *"Jeet kune do is an offensive art rather than a defensive one."*

I was startled and confused by his declaration. "Do you mean," I asked, "that we should throw the first punch?"

Lee shook his head. He explained that the JKD practitioner must strike while the opponent is preparing to attack or when he indicates his intention to attack.

Noticing the perplexed look on my face, Lee motioned for me to come forward so he could demonstrate the principle. He had me chamber my fist to deliver a rear punch, and as I drew back, he hit me.

He then instructed me not to telegraph my techniques. "Just assume the posture you would be in prior to throwing the punch," he said.

I decided to try again. I shifted my weight from one foot to the other and clenched my fists. Once again, he hit me. "This time, I intercepted your attitude," he said.

Lee explained that you should always strive to intercept your opponent's attack before he launches it—or at the very latest, while he's doing it. Intercepting is the *jeet* in jeet kune do, he said. Sadly, this principle and the training methods needed to master it are rare today. I sometimes see JKD practitioners wait for their opponent to attack before countering the technique. And at that point, it's often too late.

Recreating Bruce

Having trained with Bruce Lee for nearly three years made Jerry Poteet a logical choice to tutor Jason Scott Lee for his role in *Dragon: The Bruce Lee Story*. Much of their time together on the set entailed going over Bruce Lee-style basic moves and footwork, as well as hours during which Poteet's wife Fran drilled the actor in the best methods for wielding the *nunchaku*. That did not present much of a challenge, Jerry Poteet says, because Jason was so naturally athletic that he ended up performing all his own martial arts scenes except those that involved front flips and back flips.

The *jeet kune do* instructor also reminisced about the legend's martial arts philosophies to help the young star understand the essence of the man he was portraying. "I told him about Bruce's attitudes and the integrity of the individual, and that Bruce was as good as his word," Poteet recalls.

For example, Lee believed that many people who do the martial arts just execute a kick or punch without becoming one with the technique, Poteet says. "He called it the difference between doing—where if you're kicking, you're just kicking—and being—where you *are* that kick. Once I got that across to Jason, he fit right into the role." —*Editors of Black Belt*

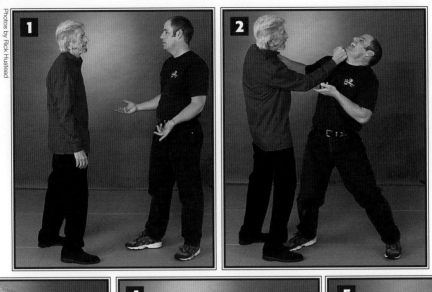

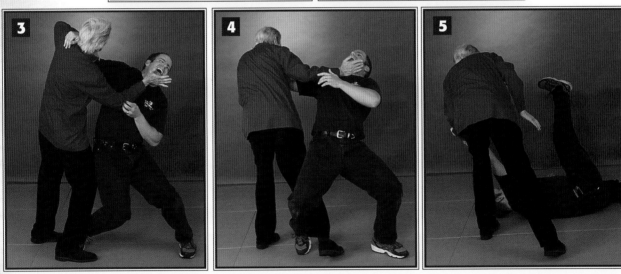

Jerry Poteet (left) focuses his visual awareness on his opponent and senses an impending attack (1). When the man extends his right arm, Poteet uses his tactile awareness and responds with a punch to the chin (2). He follows up with a palm to the jaw (3) and a sweep to the floor (4-5).

To fully appreciate this concept, which I call ATA, or attack-the-attack, imagine allowing an assailant to shoot at you before starting to defend yourself. You may get lucky and avoid the bullet, then be able to incapacitate him. Then again, you may end up dead. Not only does this passive fighting strategy violate the cornerstone principle of jeet kune do, which is to always intercept the attack, but it also puts you at least a full beat behind your opponent. Unless you're blessed with superhuman speed and are facing an unskilled opponent, this is an unwise course of action because you're forced to play catch-up. (Note, however, that it's acceptable to use a passive move to attack by drawing as you jockey around your opponent to find a position to score.)

The goal of jeet kune do is to close the distance between yourself and your opponent and smother his attack with your own. It isn't complicated, but it requires a high level of visual and tactile awareness to master.

Open Your Eyes

Visual awareness facilitates medium- and long-range fighting. It requires you to be aware of every gesture or motion your opponent makes, such as shifting his weight from one foot to the other, bending his knees or drawing his hand back. According to Lee, any of those movements can be precursors to an assault. If you can see what he intends to do, you can head him off at the pass. Furthermore, you won't be distracted by an aggressor who feints or tries to nail you with a sucker punch.

Unfortunately, many martial artists fail to train to improve their visual awareness. Even practitioners with extremely fast kicks and punches often get bested by a slower opponent because they lack visual speed, and they're too slow to react to him, let alone intercept his strikes.

To help us develop visual awareness, Lee would stand in front of the class and make a variety of gestures. Every time he moved, we had to say, "Ooh." At first, his movements were obvious—such as a punch or kick—but over time, they became more subtle—like a shift in balance or a twitch of a finger. We learned to become aware of even the slightest motion our opponent made, and that served as our cue to intercept the incoming technique. Since everybody telegraphs his attack, Lee told us, the ability to spot these motions can keep a martial artist at least a half beat ahead of his opponent.

See With Your Hands

Another important component of the ATA principle is tactile awareness or touch. Utilized at close-contact range, it refers to the pressure that develops as the other person attacks you and to your ability to use it to find an opening in his defenses. The uncanny ability of Lee and other skilled JKD practitioners to employ this method to detect and stop an assault in its tracks can make them seem psychic.

Audio Awareness

In addition to visual- and tactile-awareness drills, Bruce Lee employed audio-awareness training methods to quicken his students' reflexes. He would stand behind one of us while holding a set of clickers or sticks. Then he would hit them together, and we would execute a predetermined string of techniques as long as we heard a sound. Then he would stop the noise—usually in the middle of a sequence. If we didn't immediately halt our actions, we knew we had a lot of work to do. —J.P.

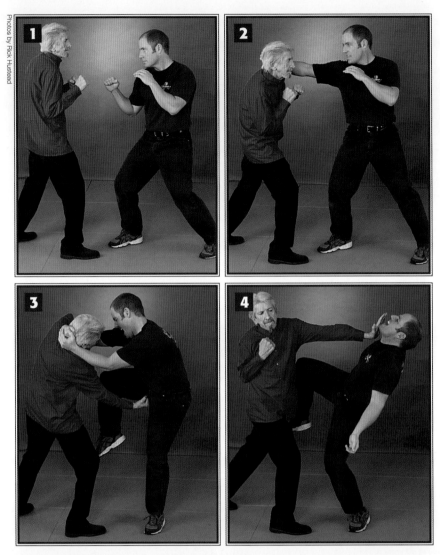

Photos by Rick Hustead

A grappler (right) accosts Jerry Poteet (1). When the man lays his right hand on the *jeet kune do* expert, he prepares his plan of attack (2). When the assailant opens himself up by reaching out with his left hand, Poteet unleashes a punch to the groin (3). He rises to a more upright stance to deliver a barrage of palm heels to terminate the aggression (4).

Lee advocated *chi sao* (sticky hands) drills to make tactile awareness more reflexive. Such training is done primarily by crossing hands with your opponent so you learn what happens if you exert too much or too little pressure.

"In the softness, you want to give without yielding," Lee would say. "Hardness is like steel that is hidden in silk." If you're too strong, the other person will dissolve his movement and attack. If you're too soft, he'll run right over you.

Many other fighting styles, including Greco-Roman wrestling, employ similar sensitivity drills. While this training method has great implications for neutral-izing grappling attacks, you should never let skill in it convince you to play the grappler's game and voluntarily go to the ground. As he tries to close the distance and grab your legs to take you down or get you in a lock, you should stop his onslaught with a straight blast.

Sensitivity drills are also a staple of old-time boxing, and they form the core of JKD's modified boxing techniques. You should practice blocking and parrying jabs and combinations to get used to them. As you become more advanced, however, you should try to intercept your partner's jab and cut through his block with your own—in true jeet kune do fashion.

Enjoy the Advantages

As you can see, the ATA principle can be used against any type of offense. For example, if an assailant attempts a punch or kick, you can intercept his technique with your own attack. If he tries to take you down, you can hit him or kick him before he succeeds. Don't waste precious time blocking, parrying and slipping when you can beat him to the punch.

When Bruce Lee named his art the "way of the intercepting fist," he meant it. And who are we to argue with the master?

The goal of *jeet kune do* is to stop an attack before it's launched. If that's not possible, it should be intercepted as early as possible during its execution.

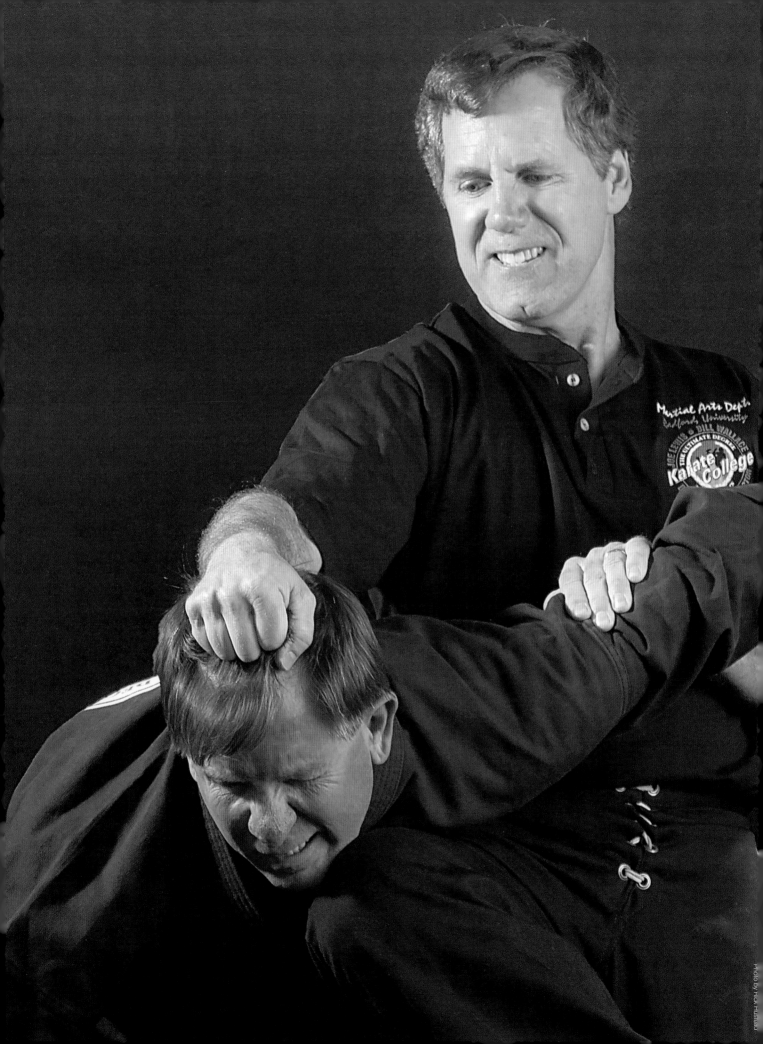

截 拳 道

On Philosophy, Jeet Kune Do and Mixed Martial Arts

by Jerry Beasley, Ed.D. — July 2005

I t's funny how the path to truth takes many curves.

Sitting in Dr. Grover's philosophy class in the spring of 1973, I was more concerned with job offers after graduation than with his lecture about Indian gurus and mysticism. That was the day I let the potential influence of Jiddu Krishnamurti on Bruce Lee's *jeet kune do* completely escape me.

At the time, I was very much an advocate of classical martial arts, tradition, organizational structure, discipline and all the other things that Krishnamurti, an Indian spiritual leader and philosopher, opposed. That same summer, I was able to see for the first time a movie starring Lee. It was *Enter the Dragon*, and it had just been released to theaters. Years passed before I made the connection.

In 1969 my karate instructor invited me to travel with him to Washington, D.C., to compete in a national tournament featuring Joe Lewis, Chuck Norris and a guy he'd been enthused about: Bruce Lee. I didn't go because I had to work.

As I think back, I wish I'd gone to the tournament. More important, if I'd paid attention in my senior philosophy class, I might have made the connection between Lee and Krishnamurti much sooner.

According to his wife Linda Lee Cadwell, Lee severely injured his back in 1970. During his three-month recovery, he studied the works of Krishnamurti.

Evolution of Mixed Martial Arts

- **1950s** World War II veterans and Asian masters introduce the martial arts to the United States.
- **1960s** Americans mix stand-up styles in competitions.
- **1970** Joe Lewis introduces full-contact kickboxing.
- **1973** The Bruce Lee persona draws thousands to martial arts training.
- **mid-1970s** Americans win kickboxing/full-contact karate titles and receive recognition.
- **1980s** Top masters from around the world immigrate to the United States for economic benefits, and many arts compete for attention. People wonder, Which art is best?
- **1993** Brazilian no-holds-barred competitions are introduced in the United States, pitting art against art.
- **mid-1990s** American wrestlers, including Dan Severn and Mark Coleman, prove the efficiency of grappling arts outside the limits of the martial arts.
- **late 1990s** American athletes, including Tito Ortiz and Chuck Liddell, prove the efficiency of striking outside the limits of the martial arts.
- **2000s** The concept of art vs. art proves inefficient. Today's MMA fighter combines boxing, kickboxing, grappling, fitness and nutrition for success. —J.B.

As his wife pointed out in *Bruce Lee: The Man Only I Knew*, he didn't just read the books. Rather, he "underlined key passages or scribbled comments in the margins." He quickly became a convert and adapted Krishnamurti's philosophy to JKD. After 1970, Lee was a changed man, and his art reflected the change.

Music buffs might recall that Beatles lead-guitarist George Harrison had a similar indoctrination to Indian mysticism. He became a student of Hindustani *sitar* guru Sri Ravi Shankar and made significant changes to his musical compositions and playing style to reflect his new adherence to Hindu spiritual beliefs. By 1970, The Beatles had completely changed their musical direction. It seems that a similar experience happened with Lee.

Ever wonder why Lee would write (in his personal notes edited by John Little), "I never wanted to give a name to the kinds of Chinese *gung fu* that I have invented"? Or when asked, "What is jeet kune do?" he said without hesitation, "Chinese martial art, definitely!" From 1968 to 1970, JKD was very much a Chinese martial art. "Reason for not sticking to *wing chun*," Lee wrote (personal notes), "because I sincerely feel that my style has more to offer regarding efficiency." He'd created a style he called jeet kune do, and he had every intent to teach his style to others.

Students who studied with Lee between 1968 and 1970 learned the art of jeet kune do. Lee's students can tell you how their classes began, how they were taught to perform a JKD kick, how they executed hand strikes and so on. Some were promoted by the Jun Fan Gung Fu Institute to various ranks in JKD based on years of training.

In stark contrast, Lee's 1971 article for *Black*

Belt, titled "Liberate Yourself From Classical Karate," is immersed in Krishnamurti philosophy. At that point, JKD had evolved from a nonclassical Chinese martial art to what Krishnamurti described in 1929 as a "pathless land." In the *Black Belt* article, Lee stated, "I have not invented a new style, composite or modification. … There is no series of rules or classification of techniques that constitutes a distinct 'jeet kune do' method of fighting."

Apparently, Lee wrote the above passages in compliance with Krishnamurti's belief that "truth being limitless, unconditioned, unapproachable, by any path whatsoever, cannot be organized; nor should any organization be formed to lead or coerce people along any particular path."

Lee was so convinced Krishnamurti held the ultimate truth that in 1971, he reversed his earlier interest in opening a chain of gung fu schools, claiming (in his personal notes), "I do not believe in schools." He went on to announce, "I have disbanded all the schools of jeet kune do because it is very easy for a member to come in and take the agenda as 'the truth' and the schedule as 'the way.' "

After 1971, JKD became the philosophy of liberation from classical arts. The "new" JKD promoted the Krishnamurti philosophy that opposed the establishment of a JKD style. By emphasizing liberation from all styles, Lee's new JKD advocated the practice of communal systems in which no style could be dominant because no style could represent the truth. This way of thinking might have helped open the door for the development of the now-popular mixed martial arts.

Nonclassical Mixed-Style Martial Arts

It's been recorded that in 1962, a young Bruce Lee was instructed by Wally Jay to improve his classical wing chun system by incorporating other martial arts to discover where their strengths and weaknesses lay. To attack where other systems are weak requires a passionate search for answers.

The early JKD was indeed a mixed-style martial art. Lee had integrated skills from wing chun, boxing, fencing and Shaolin fighting in nonclassical jeet kune do and sought to develop counters to more than a dozen other arts.

In accordance with Krishnamurti thought, it follows that JKD as truth cannot be taught. You must experience JKD to understand it; hence, the JKDism, "My truth is not your truth." In *Tao of Jeet Kune Do*, Lee tells us that to experience JKD, you must first seek truth in combat. What we know as truth in combat comes from actual physical confrontation. The message was simple: Be prepared to investigate arts or fighting methods from many teachers representing many cultures.

Step two, according to Lee, was to experience and "master the truth" at each

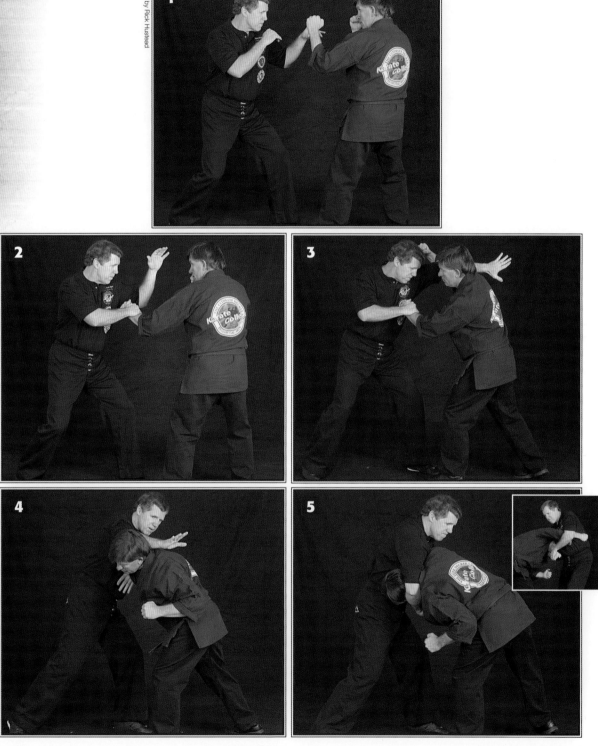

Photos by Rick Hustead

In this sequence, Jerry Beasley is unconstrained by the style. He traps his opponent's forward hand (1-2) and sets up a trap for his right cross (3). The opponent attempts to pull out of the trap (4) but is overcome by the author's superior positioning, which results in a neck crank (5).

range. In other words, be prepared to box with the boxer, kick with the kicker and go to the mat with the grappler. The next step requires that we "forget the carrier of the truth." The all-too-frequent trap facing the JKD stylist is becoming so enamored with a single art that an attachment is formed. The fighter feels the need to become identified with the art and becomes bound to the expression of that art. JKD is intended to be freedom from the bondage resulting from style identification. Remember that Lee was referring to his Krishnamurti influence here, not to his pre-1970 martial art.

Lee believed it was important to "forget the carrier of the truth" to avoid the limitations of each art. When one has spent months, even years, studying Brazilian *jiu-jitsu* or *muay* Thai, for example, it's indeed difficult to simply discard the art. Lee argued that to become JKD, one must discard the attachment to any art, even JKD. Jeet kune do, he thought, was like a boat. Its usefulness is in crossing the water. Once on the other side, the boat must not be carried on one's back.

The final step in the Krishnamurti-inspired JKD evolution is to "repose in the nothing." An example was given of Lee tossing his wallet at a student. Lee would then ask, "What style did you use to avoid being struck by the wallet?" The student's response would invariably be "no way." JKD is to simply respond. In this reference, JKD is not an art but a fighting philosophy. Some have called this way of researching and evaluating arts for personal use "the JKD concept."

The Principle Is No Principle

Lee was among the first to discover that the best way to compete against other styles is to be limited to no particular style. He found that the principles others would follow could be discarded. His art, jeet kune do, was defined as the way of no way. The difference between having no form and having no-form, he found, was like comparing a beginner who lacks form to a mentor whose form is limitless.

To achieve formlessness, one must examine a number of possible technique variations to discover that there's an unlimited number of ways to perform even a simple technique. A backfist, for example, can be viewed in the Japanese way, the Chinese way, the Korean way and so on. Lee discovered that there's no one best way to perform a skill but that the skill must be perfectly suited for the immediate need.

Any successful skill performance must be a personal expression, not an attempt to make a classical skill fit the circumstances. Lee's phrase "to float in totality" can be used to identify the sum of all the variations of the technique you've mastered. To float in totality means you make no conscious choice about which is the best way to respond. You simply respond like an echo, Lee would say. An echo offers precision because it doesn't have to make a conscious choice.

When you make a choice, it's because you recognize a limitation. An echo doesn't "think" about how it will respond. It simply responds. To use no way as way, you also must simply respond. How do you respond to a throat grab? You might use your hands to grapple or strike. You might kick. Anything goes! A classical art has structure. To use an art, you must make the skill fit the situation. To employ post-Krishnamurti JKD, you simply use what works.

Here, again, I'm interpreting JKD/Krishnamurti-based thought as a concept or philosophy. If you use this same approach, the skills and methods you eventually choose might be very different from the skills I select. This formula might work for some, but the masses want organization. Indeed, the concepts of character development, discipline and the *bushido* code must be bypassed so as not to interfere with individual expression.

Meanwhile, in the '60s ...

According to Lee, the "blind following of tradition" was the plague that limited the individual freedom of expression for the martial artist in pursuit of self-defense expertise. The tournament fighters of the late '60s had discovered that for their needs—winning in open competitions—the classical or traditional approach had certain limitations.

Often, it was argued that the way a classical art is taught and performed in the *dojo* has little to do with the way the fighter expresses himself in competition or even in self-defense. In the dojo, rules of conduct were to be followed at all costs. On the street or the tournament floor, rules of conduct often were discarded by necessity. Toss out the rules, and you might as well toss out the traditional techniques.

Tournament fighters like Norris and Lewis had discovered that if they pulled techniques from different arts, they'd be better prepared to face different types of competitors. Lewis combined the art of jeet kune do and principles of tournament karate to create American kickboxing in 1970. Once the competitors discovered that fighting with full contact didn't result in death, as the Asian masters had implied, the stage was set for a paradigm shift to mixed-martial arts competition.

Mixed Martial Arts

Modern-day mixed martial arts is the full expression of JKD when applied to an arena-fighting situation. The MMA competitor is provided with a boxing coach, a kick (boxing) coach, a grappling coach and an adviser for fitness and

In trapboxing range (1), Jerry Beasley immobilizes Floyd Burk's lead hand (2). The opponent fires back with a right cross, which is also stopped (3). With both arms immobilized (4), Beasley controls the opponent's offense (5-6). He can strike to the body (7) and head (8) until a submission is achieved. The sequence represents no particular art but contains elements of *jeet kune do* and mixed martial arts.

nutrition. Those five elements form the foundation of MMA. The end result is that the fighter experiences the truth in each range and has no problem "forgetting the carrier of truth."

The ideal MMA fighter is bound to no art because he identifies with no art. MMA is almost everything Lee spoke about more than three decades ago, yet it can be argued that it developed independently of the influence of Lee, Krishnamurti and JKD.

The practice of cage fighting had been popular in Brazil for decades. The Gracies introduced the mixed-style format in the United States in 1993 with no prior knowledge of Lee's research and innovation. Their concept was to compare one fighting system to another. The idea that one style would prove superior held true for the first year.

As soon as American wrestlers like Dan Severn and Mark Coleman, who introduced the "ground and pound" method, entered the competitions, the general approach to training changed. The wrestlers were experienced athletes. They needed only to add striking, kicking and submission skills to develop a well-rounded style.

Quickly, the format of MMA changed from art vs. art to man vs. man. As Lee had suggested—and as MMA competition proved—the individual is always more important than the art he expresses.

On Philosophy

When Lee was alive, most of the black belts I knew identified JKD as a full-contact, kickboxing style of kung fu. In the early '80s, I was able to take seminars in what was called the JKD concept. I was told that JKD was not an art but a concept. Yet I remember when it was, in fact, an art.

How can it be an art and a philosophy or concept? The answer apparently has been too obvious to ascertain. JKD was, in fact, an art. It wasn't until Lee discovered Krishnamurti that he elected to distance himself from accepted martial arts methodology and pave a new path for JKD. Lee said this very thing in his 1971 *Black Belt* article.

The art of jeet kune do is a nonclassical, mixed-style martial art that has much to offer the student. The Krishnamurti-inspired JKD philosophy has been a source of confusion. As Lee proclaimed: "Only one of 10,000 can handle it. It is silly to think almost anyone can learn it." (Little) In following this path to personal liberation, Lee partially developed a model that predated contemporary MMA by perhaps 30 years. Now that we have MMA, we can, as Lee requested, discard the boat named JKD. MMA methodology can easily be applied to self-defense.

Whether in a mixed-martial arts contest or a *jeet kune do* street fight, the opponent's energy often dictates the best choice of counters. In this sequence, the attacker's jab is immobilized (1-2). The attacker follows with a right cross (3), after which the author sets up an immobilization (4). The opponent's forward energy is used against him as the author positions himself for a leg sweep (5). He then tosses the man to the ground (6-7).

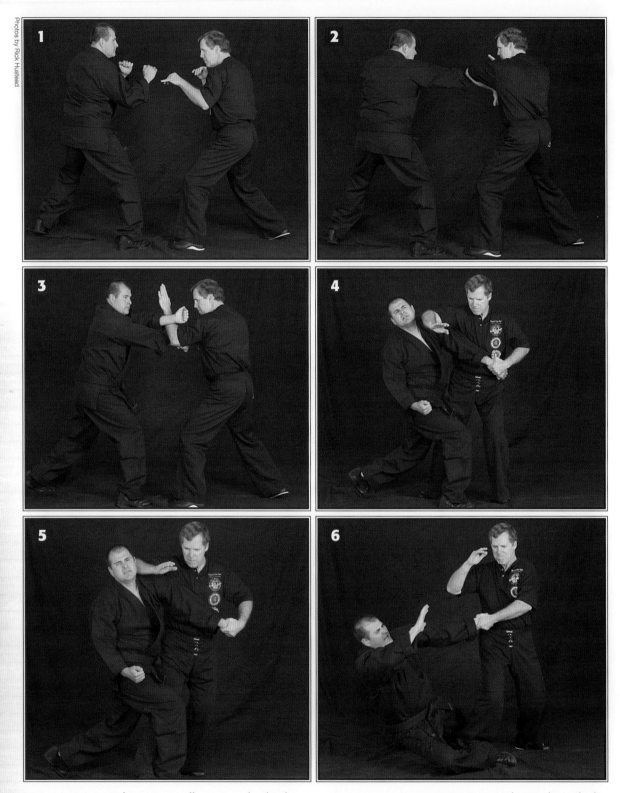

Interceptions, redirections, elbows and takedowns are common to many arts; *jeet kune do* includes them all while being limited to none. Using a typical karate-style interception (1-2) and redirection (3), Jerry Beasley follows with a Thai elbow strike (4). He then off-balances opponent Rudy Corrales with a sweep (5) and effects a takedown (6).

I've spent many years trying to make sense of the original-art-vs.-concept controversy. Was JKD always a concept, or are those who claim it was a valid art correct? It seems clear that before Lee's adoption of the way of Krishnamurti in 1970, JKD was intended to be an art. Perhaps if I'd listened to my philosophy professor that spring day in 1973, I could have solved this riddle in a more timely manner. Funny how the path to truth takes many curves.

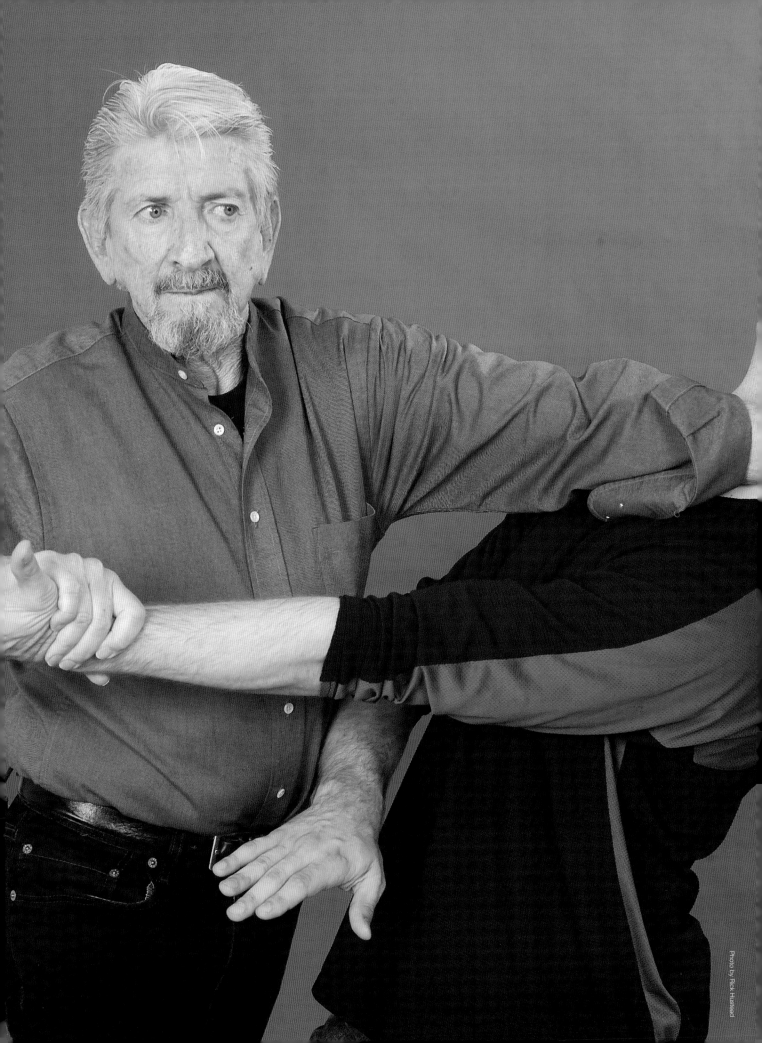

截 拳 道

To Feel Is to Believe!
Why Chi Sao Energy Training Matters

by Jerry Poteet — December 2006

O f all the expressions my teacher, Bruce Lee, was fond of using, the one that stands out the most in my memory is, To feel is to believe. Perhaps it's so memorable because he would always say it right after he hit me several times in our *jeet kune do* class.

Lee's saying embodies the reason jeet kune do students do energy training, also known as *chi sao*. Simply put, it's because your eyes can deceive you. If you visually interpret an attack at close range, you may not be able to react until it's too late. And you can be fooled by feints. It's also because your ears can misunderstand intent.

But to *feel* is to believe. If you can respond to an attack with a heightened sense of touch, you'll gain at least one beat of time. That's because you'll have eliminated the need to:

- detect that an attack is incoming,
- recognize the nature of the attack (Is it a hook, a shoot or a kick?) and
- choose the proper counter.

Even if you have twice the speed of your opponent, having to detect, recognize and choose slows you down and renders you vulnerable. It thus becomes obvious why the chi sao element of JKD is so critical in a fight. There is, however, a higher purpose to tactile-awareness training in JKD that ultimately makes it a tool for self-discovery and understanding.

The Basics

First, the thesis statement: It's in energy training that the foundation and fundamental philosophies of jeet kune do are found. In fact, Lee called chi sao and energy training "the core of JKD." Within it are economy of motion, simplicity, aggressive attack instead of passive defense, and more attributes and qualities that define the art's intercepting character.

Before preceding, one must define "energy." Simply put, it's pressure. Once you've made physical contact with your opponent, you can feel his intention. You learn to flow or "fit in" with his force or movement by developing second-nature reflexes. That's the purpose of energy training. You start in arm range, then continue to leg range and ground range. Ultimately, you expand that heightened awareness to include any thought or emotion your opponent has.

If that sounds mystical, you can bring it up with any martial artist who trained with Lee or saw him move against an opponent. He'll swear that it seemed like Lee could read his opponent's mind. And in some respects, he could because chi sao left him with an expanded awareness of all ranges of combat.

Universal Skill

Energy training can be found in many martial arts, including judo, *jujutsu*, Greco-Roman wrestling and *aikido*. All of them teach fighting methods that mirror JKD's principle of using the opponent's energy against him and yielding to a stronger force. But unlike those other arts, in JKD your offense *is* your defense. You intercept with a hit rather than first absorbing a strike and then counterattacking.

Lee learned energy training, in the form of chi sao, from the art of *wing chun* kung fu. He then modified the skills before he started teaching them to a select few private students. I was lucky enough to be one of those students. I quickly concluded that Lee considered this part of training essential to a martial artist's growth, which is probably why he taught it at his house. There, I found myself in complete awe of chi sao and all its implementations.

All the while, I knew it was just the tip of the iceberg. Lee told me that eventually I would understand. He said, "Jerry, someday you'll be driving in your car, doing some daily task, and it will hit you."

He was right. There's so much more to energy training than meets the eye. Once you understand it and can use it physically, you'll have expanded your perceptual awareness. And energy training can take you even higher: The skills you gain through physical training can transcend the martial arts and benefit you in other areas of your life.

Practical Application

JKD's first lessons in energy training come from chi sao, a double-arm exercise designed to develop sensitivity. At its highest level, it focuses on simplicity: You stick to your opponent and attack where he isn't. Where there is "emptiness," or the lack of pressure, you simply hit.

Lee believed that without chi sao and energy drills, so-called "trapping hands" exercises were little more than sequences of memorized techniques. When the average person attempts it today, he resembles a dog paddling in the water. Most of the emphasis is mistakenly placed on beating up the other person's arms—which is why many people claim that trapping doesn't work. Without a foundation in

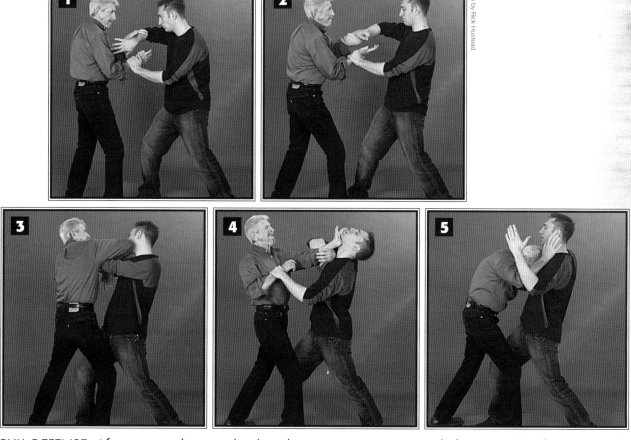

Photos by Rick Hustead

PULL DEFENSE: After approaching each other, the opponents engage with their arms (1). The man on the right pulls (2), and Jerry Poteet responds by moving in the same direction and executing an elbow smash (3). Poteet then sends a palm strike into the man's chin (4), followed by a "head spear" to the chest (5).

energy training, trapping will never work.

But Lee certainly made it work. He would often employ trapping to shut down an opponent without even hitting him. It's a more sophisticated method of fighting, one that causes many martial artists to resort to using their gross-motor skills instead of their fine-motor skills.

Basic Drills

Before you begin to implement the training exercises that accompany this article, it bears repeating that chi sao, or any other form of energy training, starts in the arms and gradually moves to the legs and the entire body. Knowing that at the outset will improve the efficiency of your workouts.

Once you understand how to generate the required pressure on a physical level, you can move on to the next phase of awareness: applying the sensitivity, without

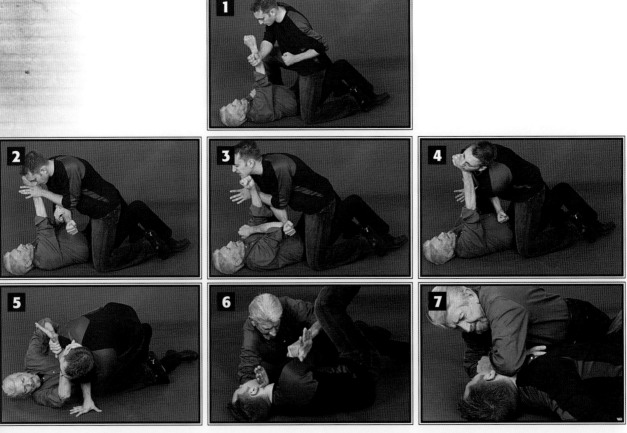

CROSS-PARRY DEFENSE: Having mounted his victim and attempted a strike, the assailant finds his blow intercepted by Jerry Poteet's punch (1). The attacker cross-parries the blow (2), which leaves an opening for Poteet's left punch (3). The *jeet kune do* teacher executes a *lap sao*/backfist to the face (4). He grabs the man's neck with his right hand and pulls his arm with his left (5). As the opponent rolls, Poteet "slices" into his neck with his right arm (6), then scrambles to the top and finishes with an elbow strike (7).

Photos by Rick Hustead

ARM-BLAST SHOOT DEFENSE: Jerry Poteet (left) confronts his opponent, who's assumed a low stance in preparation to shoot in (1). The opponent closes the gap and passes Poteet's right arm (2). Poteet counters with an elbow to the chin (3) and an open-hand strike to the neck (4) before finishing with an overhand punch to the neck (5).

making contact, to intercept your opponent's mental intention. That represents the highest expression of interception in the art of jeet kune do. To intercept once your opponent has begun his motion makes you reactive. To intercept his intention makes you proactive, but that can happen only after you've attained a higher level of awareness. You no longer have to wait for his movement; you can intercept his intention to attack.

This progressive method of enhancing tactile awareness not only creates a more efficient fighter but also makes a more aware and intelligent human being. And that's ultimately in line with the martial arts, which are intended to function as a means to examine oneself in relation to the workings of nature's laws. Jeet kune do is the art of being rather than just an art of doing, to paraphrase its founder. And energy training is philosophy in motion—a learning tool human beings can use to ultimately achieve a higher state of awareness.

截 拳 道

The Jeet Kune Do Leg Obstruction:
An Original Bruce Lee Student
Weighs In to Teach It Right!

by Bob Bremer — March 2007

The leg obstruction is one of the most important and useful tools in the *jeet kune do* arsenal, but from what I've seen recently, it's also one of the least known.

I find this very difficult to understand because the leg obstruction was one of the first techniques Bruce Lee taught at his Los Angeles school. In fact, his printed lesson plan shows that the move was included in each new student's fourth class.

I can remember the leg obstruction being taught often, and we all spent a lot of time practicing it. I admit that it's awkward to learn at first, and consequently a lot of students eventually gave up on it. I believe, however, that they made a mistake because abandoning the technique means a martial artist is electing to leave out one of the main tools of jeet kune do.

One reason the leg obstruction is so important is its versatility. It can be used effectively for offense and defense. Because the essence of jeet kune do is attacking, I'll begin my description of the technique by explaining how to use it offensively.

Photos by Rick Hustead

Jeet kune do instructor Tim Tackett (right) and Jeremy Lynch square off at fighting measure, or just far enough apart so neither person can touch the other (1). Tackett bridges the gap and, because no defensive technique is launched, executes a straight lead punch (2).

When Tim Tackett (right) attempts to bridge the gap with a straight lead punch, his opponent intercepts it with a stop-kick before he can enter striking range (1-2).

To prevent the stop-kick, Tim Tackett (right) slides forward and attacks his adversary with a leg obstruction (1-2). Once the technique is in place, the opponent can no longer punch or kick. Tackett then follows up with a straight lead punch to the jaw (3).

Attack Plans

Lee taught that there are five basic ways to attack an enemy. He assimilated them from the teachings of Western fencing. The five ways are not all equal; they're intended to work against different types of opponents. The following is the breakdown:

- **Single Direct Attack** This type of attack is designed to enable you to hit an opponent with a single technique—for example, a punch or kick. To use it successfully, you must be faster than the other person or you must be capable of striking out at the precise moment he allows himself to be physically or mentally off-balance. Jeet kune do advocates using the single direct attack in situations in which you're able to pick up on your opponent's intention or preparation—at which time you can nail him with a stop-hit or stop-kick.

- **Attack by Combination** This method relies on more than one punch or kick to defeat the opponent. It's often used after your initial hit lands or in situations in which he blocks your first technique or uses distance to escape from it.

- **Progressive Indirect Attack** This form of offense starts with a feint, which is followed immediately by a single direct attack. The strategy works best against an opponent who likes to block feints or use distance to escape from them. Caution: Don't try it on a jeet kune do practitioner because as soon as you execute the feint, he'll intercept you with a stop-hit or stop-kick.

- **Hand-Immobilization Attack** This strategy has you trapping your opponent's hand to create a momentary opening that allows you to strike.

- **Attack by Drawing** To use this method, you leave an opening for your opponent to attack so you can intercept it. It works well against martial artists who prefer to take the first shot.

Indirect Attacks

In *Tao of Jeet Kune Do,* Bruce Lee wrote, "Feinting is characteristic of the expert fighter." Good feints or indirect attacks can lead to flash knockouts because, if your opponent bites heavily on the bait, he may be totally open and unprepared for the follow-up that catches him off-guard. A good feint can cause him to walk right into a follow-up that hits like a pile driver. Indirect attacks can also be used to gradually pick apart your opponent with sharp, accurate blows that eventually reduce his resistance and defensive abilities. They weaken his body for the final blow or combination.
—William Holland

Weapon Deployment

In all strikes, your weapon should be deployed before the rest of your body, thereby saving the maximum amount of rotation and power for the moment of impact. The movement of your hips, torso, legs and shoulders is unleashed just as your weapon makes contact; it allows the payload of power from your body to be dumped on your opponent's body and not wasted en route.
—William Holland

Applying the Tactic

The success of any attack ultimately depends on the type of opponent you're facing. As an example, consider a single direct attack with a straight lead punch. You begin in the jeet kune do stance at "fighting measure," or the distance at which you must stand to remain just out of your opponent's reach. (To touch him, you have to take a step forward, which gives him time to counter.) Then you execute a straight lead punch to the head. The basic problem with this sequence is that your opponent may use a side kick aimed just below the knee to fend off your fist. See the photo sequence for details.

The only real way to be safe from this stop-kick is to obstruct it so your opponent can't use it against you. Lee taught that if you want to hit someone with a straight lead punch, you're better off using a leg obstruction first. You start at fighting measure, then attack with the leg obstruction. That opens the door for the straight lead punch to finish him.

The main reason the leg obstruction is so effective is its speed. It's fast because it doesn't require any chambering of the leg. Instead, your foot rises straight up from the floor until it makes contact just under your opponent's knee. As illustrated in the photos, you can follow up by trapping your adversary's hands and punching him. The punch will also be quick because when you effect the leg obstruction, your shoulders are square, and that ensures that your hand is already cocked.

If you do the leg obstruction correctly, you can beat your opponent's stop-hit by preventing it from landing. It can also be used to defend against other hand and leg techniques—such as the boxer's jab (left to right stance) and the *karateka* rear-leg front kick.

The information presented in this article constitutes but a few examples of how useful the leg obstruction can be. Anyone who's serious about jeet kune do should practice it until the movement is automatic.

Importance of Intercepting

Bruce Lee named his approach to fighting *jeet kune do*, which means "way of the intercepting fist." And although he later said he wished he'd never given his art a name, the name itself indicates the importance he placed on counterattacking and, more specifically, intercepting.

Intercepting is the skill of attacking the opponent while he's in the middle of his own attack or preparing to attack, Lee said. Rather than backing up to avoid the assault, or blocking the attack and then launching a counterattack, the ideal JKD interception entails launching your own attack while simultaneously deflecting or evading his weapon.

The keys to successfully intercepting your adversary's attack include proper timing, perception of his intentions, angulation away from or deflection of his weapon, and using the closest weapon to strike his closest target directly and efficiently.

—*William Holland*

Jeet kune do instructor Tim Tackett (left) effects a leg obstruction (1) before trapping his foe's lead hand and punching (2).

Tim Tackett (right) prepares to fight fellow JKD stylist Jeremy Lynch (1). When Tackett tries to bridge the gap, Lynch attempts to use a stop-kick, but Tackett halts it with a leg obstruction (2).

Tim Tackett (right) demonstrates the leg obstruction against a boxer's jab (1-2).

Tim Tackett (right) faces his opponent (1). Before the man can strike, Tackett decides to initiate a leg obstruction without chambering his leg. He lifts his lead foot (2) and extends it into the closest knee (3).

截 拳 道

4-Corner Defense:
Jeet Kune Do Fundamentals for the Street

by Tim Tackett — November 2007

O ne of *jeet kune do's* basic methods for stopping a punch is the four-corner defense, a set of maneuvers designed to protect the four quadrants of the upper body by redirecting the attack and countering. While both *wing chun* kung fu and JKD use this method, they differ in their execution of it because the structure of each art is unique. Furthermore, wing chun emphasizes using a simultaneous block and hit, while JKD advocates intercepting the attack.

The key to making the four-corner defense work is to practice it from a natural stance as well as from a fighting stance. The natural stance is the best way to orient yourself if, for example, you get into the age-old argument that starts with, "Hey! Are you looking at my girlfriend?" It's good because it's nonthreatening, which means you may still be able to defuse the tension and avoid the fight. It also offers a strategic way to face a potential adversary because it positions your body at the ready without conveying any information about your defensive ability.

When you assume the natural stance, it's essential to keep your hands up and your opponent far enough away that he has to step forward to make contact with a punch. Without that buffer zone, which is called "fighting measure" in JKD circles, chances are he'll be able to hit you because of the time lag between

Tim Tackett (right) shows the fighting measure from a fighting stance. The distance prevents the opponent from reaching him unless he steps forward.

his punch and the initiation of your parry. You'll be successful at this range only if your opponent is a lot slower than you or if he telegraphs his attack. Because you can't count on either shortcoming, you need to practice maintaining a safe distance.

Blocking

Once you've honed your ability to keep the fighting measure, you'll force your opponent to take a step forward to land his attack, and that often gives you the time you need to take appropriate action. When he advances, you have to decide whether to hit him or to use footwork to keep your distance yet again. In training, create scenarios that will develop your ability to choose—specifically, have your partner play the role of someone who just wants to ask for directions

The block and hit is a viable response to a low straight lead or hook punch.

SLOW: Tim Tackett (left) demonstrates the block-and-hit method against a right roundhouse punch from a right-to-right stance (1-3).

FASTER: Tackett and partner Jeremy Lynch demonstrate the simultaneous block-and-hit against the same punch from the same stance (1-3).

FASTEST: Tackett and Lynch show the preferred method, which consists of an interception and an immediate parry (1-3).

(in which case you should maintain your distance) as well as someone who wants to assault you (in which case a strike would be appropriate).

Next, drill against various hand attacks. You should practice from a matching (right-to-right) stance and an unmatched (right-to-left) stance. In JKD, one of the first things you learn is how to defend against a right roundhouse punch or hook executed from a right-to-right stance. You practice responses from the least efficient end of the spectrum to the most efficient. The least efficient way to deal with any punch is to block and then hit because no matter how fast you are, you'll experience a time lag between your opponent's attack and your block. This is particularly true if he's good at feinting.

While the simultaneous block-and-hit method is efficient, it's been determined that moving both arms at the same time is slightly slower than hitting (intercepting) and then parrying as a safety measure. In other words, the most efficient method for dealing with a roundhouse punch is to hit by intercepting your opponent's attack before his fist makes contact.

This task is easier than you might think. The key is to let your rear foot do all the work. It should twist as quickly as possible, throwing the weight it's bearing to your front leg while maintaining your balance. The accompanying punch shouldn't mimic a boxer's jab, which is thrown with the arm. Instead, it should be a full-power straight lead. To do it properly, make your rear foot "throw" your punching arm out. Positioning your front foot at a 25-degree angle helps you gain distance and allows your hip to send its energy toward the target, and it enables you to be inside his punch without moving your foot or leaning. To best accomplish that, throw the punch out by twisting your rear foot and then parrying a split second after your fist lands. If his punch is one beat, strive to hit him on the half beat.

Foot and Hip Angles

After you've internalized the concept of intercepting, practice against the straight lead and the boxer's jab. With the straight-punch defense, the angle of your foot and hip becomes crucial to your ability to intercept. That's best illustrated by trying the movement with your foot and hip at the wrong angle. Place a rubber knife or stick on your hip with your front foot at a 45-degree angle (or more), then twist your rear foot and place 70 percent of your weight on your front leg. More than likely, the training knife will point away from the target. This means that the punch won't have enough power because your hip needs to move toward the target to get the full weight of your body behind the blow.

Another way to see how this principle works requires the addition of a second stick, which your partner slowly thrusts at the center of your body. With your

WRONG WAY: When the enemy attacks, Tim Tackett twists his hips improperly, leaving himself open to the thrust (1-2).

RIGHT WAY: This time, Tackett avoids the attack by twisting correctly with his front foot and hip at the proper angle (1-4).

Tim Tackett illustrates the *jeet kune do* method of hitting on the half beat before parrying. He uses a horizontal hook against a front-hand hook in a left-to-right stance. (1-3)

front foot at too great an angle, you'll see that the transfer of your weight doesn't put you inside the training weapon's position. As a result, you get stabbed.

Now, do the same routine with your front foot pointed where it should be and your hip moving toward the target, and you'll find yourself inside the stick. This rather small adjustment makes all the difference in your being able to intercept an attack.

Subsection to come

With that under your belt, it's time to move on to the same drill while your partner punches. Aim to hit on the half beat before parrying. Sometimes you'll find it necessary to parry on the outside of the punch and hit. That usually occurs when your opponent brings his elbow out, thus making the punch easier for you to see. This blow will usually land on the right side of your face, which means it's more efficient for you to move outside its trajectory. To do that, step forward and to the left with your front foot while moving forward with your body. If you punch at the same time, you should hit your opponent before your front foot hits the ground, thus putting more of your weight into the technique. You can hit high or low, depending on the placement of your opponent's cover hand.

In JKD, the unmatched lead is treated differently. When you're in a right lead and your opponent faces you in a left lead, place your front foot slightly outside his front foot. That gives you more time to react to his rear round kick and makes it harder for him to hit you with a front-hand hook. When your foot is outside his front foot and he throws a straight left jab at your head, simply cut into his arm with sliding leverage and hit him. For those who don't know, the term "cut" refers to the act of hitting the limb and moving it off his line of attack while you establish your own line of attack.

If, for some reason, you find yourself with your front foot inside your opponent's front foot and he throws a straight left punch at your head, step forward with your shoulders square. At the same time, cross-parry with your left hand while you use sliding leverage with your right arm, hitting him in the left eye with a finger jab.

When your opponent tries to hit you with a front-hand hook, execute a hook of your own to the inside of his punch, making sure that your forearm makes contact with his arm. Your goal is to hit him with a horizontal blow. If he tries to strike you with a low straight punch, simply parry downward as you hit high to the head.

With sufficient practice of the above-mentioned techniques, you'll be able to deal with any hand attack. Just make sure to keep enough distance between yourself and your adversary to force him to step forward before hitting you. That will give you all the time you need to react—and prevail.

截 拳 道

Jeet Kune Do Grappling:
Dan Inosanto Talks About Bruce Lee's Ground Fighting and the Direction He's Taking the Art

by Dr. Mark Cheng — March 2008

Kicking, punching, trapping and grappling—the four ranges of combat are mentioned in almost every discussion of Bruce Lee's jeet kune do. But with the exception of Dan Inosanto and the late Larry Hartsell, none of Lee's personal students has focused on the fourth range, which is ironic because grappling is all the rage these days. In this interview, Inosanto addresses the often-overlooked subject of JKD ground work, both as it was practiced during Lee's life and as it's being practiced now.

Q: A lot of people think that Bruce Lee's *jeet kune do* was only about kickboxing and trapping, but that's not the whole picture, is it?

Inosanto: Absolutely not. While *sifu* Bruce was alive, he personally researched grappling arts like Chinese *chin-na*, Wally Jay's *jujutsu* and Japanese judo, and he trained with Gene LeBell. Even in *Tao of Jeet Kune Do*, he clearly illustrated grappling techniques—throws, locks and submissions. And

Photo by Rick Hustead

Dan Inosanto practices stand-up grappling with sticks.

if you watch the opening scene of *Enter the Dragon* where he's fighting Sammo Hung, how does he finish the fight? With a submission.

Q: Why do you think that so many people can't see past Lee's kickboxing, trapping and *nunchaku* work?

Inosanto: Sifu Bruce knew what looked good on camera. [Most] of the techniques in his movies are striking oriented, not because he couldn't do other things but because he clearly knew that the subtleties of grappling are very hard, if not impossible, for the camera to capture.

Just look at mixed-martial arts bouts. In the early days of the Ultimate Fighting Championship, the referees didn't stand the fighters back up if they were inactive on the ground for too long, but the fans started booing, and the promoters had to acknowledge that the viewing public wanted to see action or else the money would go elsewhere. The action might be a little shift of the hips or fighting for grips underneath, but if the fans can't see it, they can't appreciate it. And if they can't appreciate it, they won't enjoy it.

The other reason he didn't show as much grappling in his movies is it was an area that was relatively new to him. He had tons of hours of kick, punch and trap training, but his research into the grappling arts was still in its infancy. If he was going to show something on-screen, sifu Bruce wanted to really shine at it.

But he was actively investigating the ground range, and he even started developing *chi sao* from the ground. However, during sifu Bruce's lifetime, fighting was more of a stand-up game.

Q: Was grappling a regular part of the curriculum at the Chinatown school?

Inosanto: Sifu Bruce taught locks and submissions on the ground, and take-downs, but they weren't contested. In other words, we practiced them for technical development and not in a sparring sense, like we did with kickboxing. We didn't wrestle against each other like we did with the kickboxing.

What he did do was work on certain things with individual students during his private lessons. When he taught private lessons, he'd not only focus on what might work best for individuals—their personal JKD—but also train himself at the same time, bettering his own skills in a particular range.

One of the things that made him unique was his ability to move from kicking range to punching range to trapping range to grappling range. At that time, most martial artists really shined in one particular range. If you kicked, you didn't punch or grapple much. If you punched, you didn't kick or grapple much. And if you grappled, you didn't have the same skill level in striking. Sifu Bruce was way ahead of his time in how he was training himself and his students to be adept at bridging the gap between ranges.

Q: Are there different ranges within grappling range?

Inosanto: Certainly. There's what's referred to in *Tao of Jeet Kune Do* as the tie-up range, which is essentially the standing clinch range. This is like what wrestlers do now with pummeling. They have the collar hold. They grab the biceps, triceps, wrist, neck, forearm, etc. These clinch tactics are highly useful for strikers because they allow them to tie up their opponents and gain some time to recover from a solid hit or to catch their breath. Grapplers must learn this range, or else they'll be unable to bridge the gap and dominate their opponents on the ground. So they have techniques like overhooks, underhooks and the two-on-one to help them achieve the takedown. That's a different game than the ground game, but they're both part of the totality of grappling.

Q: Did Lee teach drills that included striking on the ground?

Inosanto: No. We put those in later, after his passing, [because] of Shooto people like Yori Nakamura, who taught those to us around 1989 to 1990.

Because of working with Yori, I saw the necessity for ground work, and then later when I got into Brazilian *jiu-jitsu* with the Machado family and Renato Magno, I really saw the need for ground work.

I combined a lot of the movements from Shooto and Brazilian jiu-jitsu's *vale tudo* training with the striking, trapping and grappling that I learned from sifu Bruce and others. Not that what I'm doing is 100-percent correct, but those are the sources that make up our ground game, and we give credit for what comes from where.

We also have influences from other grappling systems—*dumog*, which I learned from Juan LaCoste; *naban*, which is the python system of *bando* as taught by Dr. Maung Gyi; and others.

Q: Bando has a grappling system?

Inosanto: Yes. There's a history lesson here. People often think that something is absent from history when they don't have exposure to it in the media, but that doesn't mean it didn't exist. Mixed martial arts have always been around. Bando, for example, has kickboxing, weapons and wrestling, but very few people knew about it before. Why now? Because there's money involved with MMA, instead of people just doing something as a cultural or family treasure.

Even on the Hawaiian sugar plantations decades ago, the Filipinos were doing MMA. They kickboxed and grappled with sticks and training daggers. Now we're more aware of it because of the TV coverage and Internet exposure.

Q: Many people say that trapping is its own separate range and is distinct from grappling. What are your thoughts?

Inosanto: Trapping is actually easier on the ground. The ground takes away one vector of motion, so it limits the opponent's motion and forces him to be really elusive. A good shootwrestler or BJJ practitioner knows all about trapping at a high level, but he doesn't necessarily call it "trapping." He might call it "clinching" or "pinning" or "holding," but all those terms reflect a form of trapping. For example, if someone underhooks your arm or grabs your arm and hits you or throws you, you got trapped. A trap doesn't have to be a *pak sao* or *lap sao* or something like that.

Q: On the ground, can you employ a variety of percussive or striking techniques?

Inosanto: Absolutely. You have to be able to flow into and out of whatever a

Photo by Rick Hustead

First-generation JKD practitioner Dan Inosanto continues to keep the legacy of *jeet kune do* alive.

Martial arts like *kali* use weapons, and the authors say that training with weapons develops body mechanics.

situation calls for or whatever energy your opponent gives you. Like I said, Brazilian jiu-jitsu is a strong trapping art, and higher-level practitioners might trap your arm and transition to a position of greater advantage and leverage, then start punching or elbowing you. You have to realize that trapping in Brazilian jiu-jitsu, for example, is about creating control of a limb to create control of the opponent's body before attempting a submission. When I was training with sifu Bruce in stand-up, he'd create a control on two of my limbs just for a moment and hit me at least two or three times per trap.

Q: Perhaps because of the earliest UFCs, there was a lot of talk about how boxing doesn't work on the ground. On the other hand, I've heard that Ray "Boom Boom" Mancini would even bob and weave on the ground. Is that true?

Inosanto: Yes. While we were training once, I was watching him hold someone in the guard when he was working on vale tudo. As the person in the guard was trying to rain down punches on him, Boom Boom bobbed and weaved until he found an opening for either his punches or a control and submission. He didn't have to be taught that. He just applied his natural instinct as a world-class boxer. You can certainly employ a great deal of what works in standing range on the ground as long as you understand the context. The clinch skills he learned as a stand-up boxer serve him very well on the ground.

Some instructors claim that it's hard to get power when striking on the ground.

Boom Boom Mancini can uppercut you in his guard, and it will seriously rattle you. It doesn't take a knockout shot each time. All you have to do is get a couple of shots in, and you'll be surprised how greatly your opponent's skill or ability level decreases. The late Carlson Gracie said that the first punch a black belt takes can turn him into a brown belt. After two punches, he becomes a purple belt, and after three punches, he's operating at a blue belt's technical level. After four, he's basically in raw survival mode.

A punch can also be a setup for another technique, like an attack-by-drawing sequence. You can use a punch as an irritant, just to get the opponent to put his arms up, which in turn can give you the opportunity to change position, gain control and make a submission.

Q: What are your thoughts on the grappling legacy of Lee?

Inosanto: My personal thought is that sifu Bruce would think that it's OK to research other grappling arts, like *shooto* and Brazilian jiu-jitsu. I think that if he'd had information on those systems, he'd have researched them to find out what was valuable.

These days, we use some of their techniques and moves in our JKD. When I teach, I always say, "This move came from shootwrestling," "This series came from *kali*," or "This move came from Brazilian jiu-jitsu." We maintain the integrity of what was passed on from sifu Bruce, while not closing our eyes to the good points of other systems.

I hold the rank of senior shooter under *sensei* Yori Nakamura, black belt in Brazilian jiu-jitsu under Rigan Machado and sixth-level black belt in bando under Dr. Maung Gyi, but regardless of those achievements, I realize that I have to be more proficient and knowledgeable. Even though I learned grappling from masters such as LaCoste, Tenio and Subing, the arts of shooto, BJJ and Erik Paulson's Combat Submission Wrestling refined my understanding of grappling.

It's like when you go to someone's house, you don't walk in the door and see that every little thing [comes] from only one store. You might see one piece of furniture, like a couch, from one store and an end table from another store. As long as the ensemble works well together visually and functionally, nobody makes a big deal out of it. That is JKD. You don't have to embrace everything that comes from one source or rely solely on one source for everything you need. What we have and what we use as individuals should be customized to our tastes and abilities. Rigan Machado said to me: "You don't embrace the entire system of BJJ but rather embrace what works for you in BJJ. You don't adapt to BJJ but take out of jiu-jutsu what adapts to you."

Some critics will say, "Don't call that 'JKD grappling,'" since what we're teaching might be only 40 percent of what sifu Bruce taught, but what worked for him might not work for you. JKD grappling is a result of research, experimentation, creation and development in order to tailor-make a system of grappling that suits the individual. It is a sharing, experimenting and learning process at my academy and is under constant evolution.

Street fighting is evolving. Back in the 1960s, nobody knew how to kick like the average street fighter does now. And nowadays, because of media exposure, the average untrained assailant is more familiar with grappling. War, conflict, combat, fighting—however you want to put it—it's in constant evolution. If your combative technology and strategies don't evolve, you risk extinction. The spirit behind JKD is still intact and very much alive, but the body and the usage of it have evolved to be aware of the entirety of combat.

截 拳 道

The JKD Professor:
Jeet Kune Do as Seen
Through the Eyes of Gary Dill,
James Lee's Most Prominent Student

by Paul J. Bax and John T. Bingham — February 2008

Gary Dill freely admits the reason for his initial attraction to the martial arts: self-defense. He had little interest in the philosophy or discipline the Asian arts offered. "I only wanted to learn how to kick someone's butt," he says.

"But as I grew older and hopefully wiser, I realized that the philosophical aspects were important to my overall development," Dill says. "Now I work on the combat arts, my *yang* side, on a daily basis, but I also work on my *yin* side, utilizing internal energy and *chi* breathing. I try to balance out my warrior spirit with both types of training."

When he started in 1963, Dill's styles of choice were karate and *jujutsu*. He didn't discover *jeet kune do* until three years later, when he spied Bruce Lee portraying Kato on *The Green Hornet*. "My perspective on the classical arts changed when I saw Kato on TV. Then *Black Belt* came out with a two-part series on Bruce, confirming his authenticity in *gung fu*," Dill says. "I found out about James Lee

Gary Dill holds a photo of his *jeet kune do* instructor, James Lee.

when I was in Vietnam and read about him in the old *Karate Illustrated* magazine in an article titled 'Special Gung Fu Training Devices.' The article indicated that James was teaching a jeet kune do class in Oakland, California, and I knew that was where I was going to be relocated to upon my return."

Once stateside, Dill tracked down James Lee. "My interfacing with James gave me the technical know-how, whereas Bruce's writings had given me the philosophical mind-set," he says. "But let me add this: James Lee's JKD class was so accelerated, so intense and so much in tune with combat [that] one would learn more in a month than many would learn in a year in a classical martial art. When I started training under him, I thought I'd died and gone to martial arts heaven. It was the best training I'd ever obtained."

While he appreciated the no-nonsense nature of JKD, Dill harbored no disrespect for the traditional arts he studied, one of which was *goju-ryu* karate under *Black Belt* Hall of Fame member Lou Angel. "I really enjoyed the hard-core sparring that went down in the 1960s in Oklahoma and Texas," he says. "I hated to do the *kata*, but they were a necessary evil for promotion. In those days, there was no sparring equipment. Everything was bare hand, and if you wanted to score a point, you'd better make some serious contact. I was fortunate to have Lou Angel as my sparring mentor, for he was and still is one mean fighting dude."

Having been promoted by Angel to instructor in October 1965, Dill was content to stick with goju-ryu until James Lee accepted him into his Oakland JKD class in 1971. The eclectic art suited him to a T. "JKD was very combat oriented, and I took to it immediately because of my background in the rough

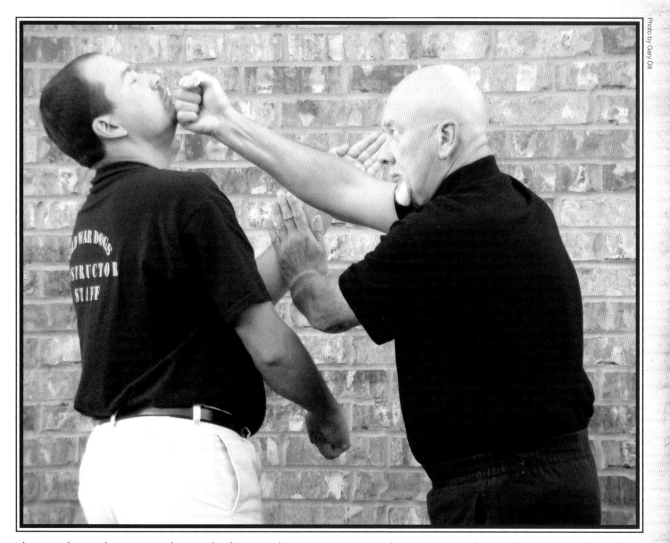

The *jeet kune do* training that took place under James Lee's tutelage was accelerated, intense and combat oriented, says Gary Dill (right).

Harmony and Unity for All

The *jeet kune do* world always seems to host more than its fair share of controversy. For a variety of reasons, practitioners and instructors had a tough time getting along after Bruce Lee passed away. "I've tried several times during the past five to six years to do my part to promote the concept of harmony and unity within JKD—as it was most aptly phrased by Taky Kimura, who is the true gentleman of JKD," Gary Dill says. "But after a while, one just gives up and moves down his own path, with his sword unsheathed. I will do my thing, my JKD, and they can do their thing. In all fairness, this type of political infighting is prevalent in all martial arts; the JKD community didn't invent it."

To further his efforts to do his thing, Dill formed the Jeet Kune Do Association in 1991. Its mission is threefold: "To preserve and maintain original JKD; to provide a structured, organized training format for JKD; and to utilize a professional certification and instructor-development program," he says. "We have 27 schools and 40 instructors, and we host seminars from coast to coast, as well as three Oklahoma training camps every year." —P.B., JTB

karate sparring of the '60s," Dill says. "What was really great about JKD [was that] there were no kata."

Classes were held in James Lee's garage twice a week and typically lasted one hour. Shoes were worn, but uniforms were not. "We started with a formal salutation, spent several minutes loosening up, and then jumped immediately into learning and practicing techniques," Dill says. "There were no breaks, no water; it was one hour of concentrated working out. James had no time for tire kickers and slackers. He was a nice guy, but he took his JKD seriously, and he expected you to do the same."

Before class began, Lee always made sure that the garage door was pulled two-thirds of the way down. One reason was that it kept passersby from peeking in. The other had to do with humility. "To enter the garage, we had to literally crawl in under the door," Dill says. "It helped deflate those of us with egos."

When Dill left Oakland, he spoke with Lee about carrying on the art and was given a lesson plan. "He sent me a three-page typewritten outline of JKD training and wrote on it that it was a good 18 to 24 months of training if taught properly," Dill says. "He also included 12 of his small, red Introduction to JKD booklets, which he gave new students when they were accepted into his garage class."

Despite Lee's low-profile approach to JKD, Dill says that his teacher wasn't overly protective of the art. "There were no secrets. He was just very cautious about who he taught. He was looking for serious, open-minded students who would give him 100 percent during the JKD workout."

And for Lee, it was the workout that mattered. Philosophy and meditation

BASIC ENTERING TO TRAPPING: From the JKD fighting stance, Gary Dill (right) faces his opponent, who's in a right lead (1). To begin the entering phase, Dill executes a right backhand strike that uses his closest weapon to attack the opponent's closest target (2). He then closes the gap with a right step, making sure he stays on the outside, and uses his left hand to trap the man's right elbow so his right fist can be launched at his face (3).

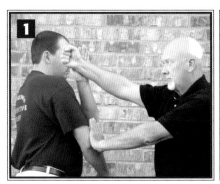  

WHAT-IF SCENARIO, RIGHT LEAD: Dill attempts the combination depicted on the first photo sequence, but the opponent parries the face punch with his left hand (1). In response, Dill removes his left hand from the man's right elbow and uses it to grab his left forearm (2). Once the limb is out of the way and restricting the movement of the man's right arm, Dill effects a snap punch to the face (3).

  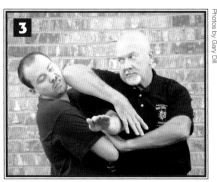

WHAT-IF SCENARIO, RIGHT LEAD: Dill tries to counter with the same punch, but the opponent stops the blow with a left open-hand block (1). He overextends his movement, pushing his arm past his own centerline (2). Following the man's energy flow, Dill sends an elbow strike over the limb while making sure his arms are pinned against his chest (3).

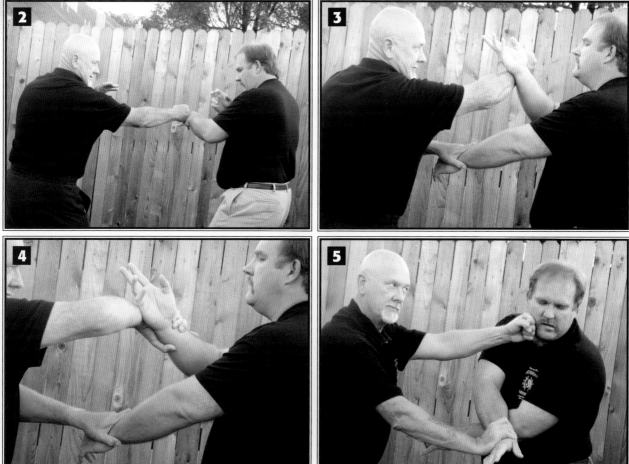

WHAT-IF SCENARIO, LEFT LEAD: Gary Dill (left) and his partner, who's in a left-lead stance, square off (1). To facilitate his entering move, Dill uses his lead hand to strike the man's lead hand (2). He then executes a right step, grabs his lead arm with his left hand and attempts to strike his face with a right backhand, but the opponent blocks it (3). Feeling the man's energy, Dill rotates his right hand and transitions to a wrist grab (4), after which he pulls the man's right arm down and across his body to pin his left limb. The JKD instructor then hits him in the face with a straight punch (5).

played no role in the training sessions. Any intangibles that were taught were combat oriented. "James frequently spoke of the importance of developing a killer instinct," Dill says. "He said that one could never become a true JKD man unless he had it. I'd just gotten back from Vietnam, [so] I understood what he meant.

"What is killer instinct? It's the ability, the desire, to take out a person who's threatening you and do it without hesitation, without any afterthought. To take care of business without any remorse. That's my definition. James never defined it. He would say that you must find your own definition, and when you did, you would know it."

Surprisingly, sparring wasn't part of the curriculum. "I don't know what happened before I got there in June 1971, but James told me that he wouldn't allow sparring in his class because of the possibility of lawsuits in case of injury," Dill says. "We were expected to spar on our own time. James taught the techniques; it was up to us to put them together. He didn't hold our hands."

Outside of class, Dill immersed himself in fighting but not with his fellow JKD students. "The guys in my group never interfaced; we all had different lifestyles," he says. "I trained in JKD while I was in the Navy. I also had my own martial arts class composed of primarily Navy and Marine Corps personnel. I had my own office and would work out several hours every day using my own students as my partners. Thanks to the U.S. Navy, I was practically a full-time JKD practitioner all the time that I trained under James. After every class with him, I made detailed handwritten notes on each technique and drill he taught that night."

Prominent in his notebook were Lee's lessons on being nontelegraphic. The term "telegraphic" describes pre-technique movements such as chambering a foot or fist before the attack, Dill says. When you telegraph a technique, your body language warns your opponent that you're ready to strike. The JKD classes emphasized developing the ability to attack without tipping off your opponent.

Students at the Oakland school engaged in sensitivity training—many of the hand techniques were presented from a one-arm, wrist-touching position, Dill says—but traditional *chi sao* wasn't part of the picture. "Here's an interesting story: James taught my group two-hand chi sao for about two to three classes. He asked us if we understood the concept. Of course, we all said yes. Then the surprise statement: 'Good, because you'll never work on it anymore.'"

James Lee said Bruce Lee had concluded that chi sao wasn't an efficient way to spend the students' time and that it had insufficient combat applicability. "He had told [James] to phase it out of the Oakland curriculum," Dill says.

One familiar face in JKD schools—the *mook jong* wooden dummy—wasn't phased out. "He definitely had one in the garage school," Dill says. "He used old-fashioned car springs across the back of it to give it bounce. He had us work on it frequently, along with other JKD training equipment he'd made."

The presence of the wooden dummy points to the importance of one of three arts that contributed to the JKD gene pool. According to James Lee, they were *wing chun* kung fu, Western boxing and fencing. Was there any talk of the art being composed of 26 or 27 styles, as some practitioners claim? "Never," Dill says. "To my knowledge, he had no interest or training in arts [such as *kali*, *escrima* or *silat*]. Remember that those arts didn't begin to get noticed on a large scale until years after Bruce and James died. From my observations, James was only into JKD as it was developed by Bruce from wing chun, boxing and fencing."

Like all good things, Dill's time with James Lee would come to an end. "I knew his days were numbered when I left Oakland and returned to Oklahoma; I knew I'd never see him again," Dill says. "I didn't know [about his death] until I read about it in *Black Belt*. I wasn't surprised, but still I was upset because he did so much for me. He was a great guy and a true warrior."

截 拳 道

Power of the Dragon:
Bruce Lee's Methods for Maximizing Your Ability to Fight

by Paul Vunak and Erin O'Toole — June 1999

I t has been some 26 years since the death of Bruce Lee, yet it is safe to say that his popularity has not diminished at all. In fact, martial artists' fascination with Lee's concepts and principles is greater than ever. Because of his TV and movie roles, there has been an amazing increase in the public's interest in the martial arts in general and *jeet kune do* in particular. Lee was able to reach a segment of the population that otherwise would not have thought about combat.

Much of the world's current interest in the martial arts also stems from the proliferation of no-holds-barred tournaments such as the Ultimate Fighting Championship. If you do your homework and look back at Lee's writings, such as *Tao of Jeet Kune Do*, it becomes clear just how ahead of his time he was; for every bit of information, every criticism of traditional styles, and every principle of combat he wrote about can be observed in the matches that take place in NHB events. Consider: How many NHB fighters use a low stance? How many traditional blocks do they employ? How many flashy kicks do they throw? Where are all the self-proclaimed grandmasters, and why didn't they bring their *chi* (internal energy)?

There are four components to power: speed, footwork, strength and body mechanics. Ted Wong (right) is pictured.

Regardless of whether you believe NHB events should be televised, one fact is indisputable: Martial artists of the 1990s are hungry for a heaping dose of reality. There is a growing movement away from the *Billy Jack* mentality that Hollywood fostered during the 1970s and '80s. It is somewhat ironic, then, that most people have become familiar with Lee through the "theatrical jeet kune do" used in his films because it is his functional style of fighting that has stood the test of time. He had the courage and tenacity to challenge what had been tradition for thousands of years. Like basketball's Michael Jordan and boxing's Muhammad Ali, Bruce Lee was decades ahead of his time.

What made Lee such an incredible fighter? It wasn't his ability to dazzle an audience with awesome kicks or complex moves. On the contrary, it was something that is not even recognizable to most people who watch his films. It was the fact that he possessed certain attributes that set him apart from the rest of the world: speed, "killer instinct," coordination, sensitivity, timing and power. While these attributes may not be as exciting as flashy kicks or a loud *kiai* (shout), they are by far the most effective and potent weapons a fighter can have in his arsenal. In fact, you can witness most of them in NHB matches—if you know what to look for.

Thousands of words could be written on the subject of functional martial arts attributes. This article will shed some light on the first, and perhaps most important, one: power.

What exactly is power, and what does it mean to you as a martial artist? According to the dictionary, power can be thought of as "strength or force actually put forth." In *Tao of Jeet Kune Do*, Lee described power as the "ability to injure a moving target." To truly understand it and develop it, it helps to identify the different aspects one needs to hit with power. Power can be broken down into four components, each of equal importance. They are speed, footwork, strength and body mechanics.

Speed

To understand speed, you must first understand that there are different kinds of speed. To define speed as simply "miles per hour" is akin to saying that Jordan is simply "coordinated." As simple as the word "speed" sounds, a student needs to have a rather complex definition of it. Think of it as the ability to close the gap between yourself and your opponent with explosiveness and economy of motion.

As any physics major can tell you, power is directly proportional to mass and velocity squared. A small piece of lead thrown at a person can inflict pain, but if the same piece of lead is hurled by a slingshot, it will inflict damage. If, however, it is propelled by 240 grains of gunpowder, it will cause instant destruction. The only factor that differentiates pain from destruction is the speed at which the lead moves.

Over the years, we've had the privilege of training with numerous fighters, ranging from the legendary Bill "Superfoot" Wallace to the more sublime Daniel Duby, the man who originally popularized *savate* in America. Being exposed to so many different styles has afforded us the opportunity to view speed from many different vantage points. To this day, the fastest man we've ever seen—and one who nearly set a world record in the 100-yard dash at 9.4 seconds—is Dan Inosanto. He is also the man who spent perhaps the most time watching the metamorphosis of Lee's speed on an almost daily basis. "Bruce just kept getting faster and faster," he says.

Lee's capacity to overwhelm an opponent depended not only on his speed but also the quickness with which he delivered his blows. In other words, he executed his techniques with impeccable economy of motion, which is a vital element of speed.

Paul Vunak says that the stick fighting art of *kali* influenced *jeet kune do.*

JKD practitioners believe all types of strength have a function on the street.

The good news is that it is possible to improve your speed. Although some people seem to have an inherent capability of being fast, speed is not purely genetic, nor is it solely a young man's game. At 85, John LaCoste could wield a *kali* stick so quickly that observers could not see it, and at 86, Helio Gracie can still get to your back and choke you out before you've counted your first sheep.

To improve your speed, select a motion or technique you would like to execute more rapidly, then break it into two parts. For example, you can break the jab into part one, which is your hand extending outward, and part two, which is your hand retracting. Next, practice only the first part over and over. This helps develop your explosiveness, or as Lee used to say, your "suddenness." It works with virtually any technique.

Footwork

"Footwork is probably one of the most important qualities a fighter can possess," Inosanto says. The ability to put your body where you want it in relation to your opponent determines the outcome of every movement—whether offensive or defensive—you launch during a fight. One problem with the martial arts is the belief that a person can concoct a stance that will hide his vital organs from attack, thereby reducing his chance of injury. The result is either a convoluted, static posture that imitates an animal or insect—with a morphology completely unlike that of a human being—or a stance that rejects mobility in favor of stability. In some cases, with a stance that positions the legs wide apart and the body low, it is difficult enough to get out of the way of a cartwheel, much less a fast jab aimed at your nose.

In Lee's quest for street reality, he and Inosanto discovered certain truths. "In long range, where punches and kicks are being thrown, one does not need stability. One needs agility to evade punches while still being able to counter-punch, kick and stop-hit without telegraphing," Lee wrote. This truth led the two martial artists to styles such as Western boxing, kali, fencing and savate—all of which have movement as their common denominator. Consequently, they make extensive use of fakes, broken rhythm and so on.

Proper footwork also ensures that when you punch or kick, your weapon will land with maximum effectiveness. The pugilist's axiom of "stick and move" applies as much to the martial arts as to boxing. Be light on your feet, then move into the correct range for the hit.

There are several ways to develop more agile footwork. Knife sparring (with a dulled blade) is one of the best methods: You and a partner put on a glove to protect your knife hand, then try to avoid being "cut." You will quickly learn that you must move swiftly to stay out of range of your opponent's weapon. Jumping rope is also an excellent method for sharpening your footwork, as is cross-training in basketball.

Strength

The third factor in maximizing power is strength. Although there are several types of strength—the strength of a rock climber is different from the strength of a bodybuilder—all should have a place in your training. Most effective for street fighting is the one called tendon strength.

Generally speaking, when you perform an exhaustive motion—a bench press or curl, for example—the reason for failure is not the muscle but the tendon. Tendons, which connect muscle to bone, can be thought of as the weak link. Most people blame only their muscles when failure occurs, but in actuality, it is the lack of tendon strength. Whenever you isolate a position for five or more seconds, you place a stress on a particular joint, thus strengthening the associated tendons. Various isometric exercises can enhance your tendon strength.

Keep in mind, however, that all types of strength have a function in a street fight. Powerlifting lends explosiveness, while bodybuilding—if not overdone—can add protective "padding" to the body, thus reducing the chance of injury. It certainly behooves you to cross-train in these different strength areas, perhaps with an emphasis on isometrics. Your strength-to-weight ratio will increase, and much like a car that has been given a stronger engine, you will move with increased power.

Body Mechanics

The final ingredient in the recipe for power is body mechanics, which refer to the perfect movements that allow you to obtain the most leverage and economy of motion. In other words, having good body mechanics means having perfect form in motion. Jordan's jump shot, Arnold Palmer's golf swing and Joe Namath's pass—these are examples of people who have mastered the body mechanics of their particular game.

Possibly one of the greatest revelations in jeet kune do occurred when Inosanto gave Lee his first kali lesson. Both men quickly realized that the body mechanics required to use the weapons were much more demanding than those needed for empty-hand techniques. When an opponent is wielding a razor-sharp 36-inch-long double-edged blade, there is an amazing proclivity for perfection of movement. Either that or you need to have plenty of sutures and bandages around.

Spend a half-hour or more every day training with weapons in front of the mirror, and in terms of developing your body mechanics, you will have put in the equivalent of five hours of ordinary shadowboxing. Your empty-hand skills will improve at a much more dramatic rate than if you were to train only empty-handed. People who regularly work out this way move with more sharpness and agility than do most others, and their body mechanics are notably above average.

Conclusion

Power is definitely an attribute you can improve. All it takes is for you to train according to the four components described above. To summarize:

- Speed: Break a particular technique into parts and practice each part separately. That will develop the explosiveness of the technique.

- Footwork: Cross-train in sports that require a lot of agility, such as basketball. Knife sparring will help you develop catlike movements.

- Strength: Let isometrics make up 60 percent of your weight training and divide the rest of your time between powerlifting and bodybuilding.

- Body Mechanics: Work with various weapons. Perform all motions at half speed and watch your movements critically in the mirror.

截 拳 道

Know Yourself Through Jeet Kune Do

by Fiaz Kareem — October 1998

"Self-knowledge is the basis of jeet kune do because it is effective—
not only for the individual's martial arts but also for his life as a human being."
—Bruce Lee

The touchstone and core philosophy of Bruce Lee was to "know your-self." It becomes clear to the more cognizant mind that all the avenues Lee took in life were in pursuit of self-cultivation, which leads to the ultimate destination: self-knowledge. His art and philosophy were the vehicles he used to gain an understanding of himself, to feel and fully appreciate the experience of what it means to be a human being. To achieve this, he spent countless hours learning, training, reading and researching.

The biggest adversary in our life is ourselves. We are what we are, in a sense, because of the dominating thoughts that we allow to gather in our head. All concepts of self-improvement, all actions and paths we take, relate solely to our abstract image of ourselves. Life is limited only by how we really see ourselves and feel about our being. A great deal of pure self-knowledge and inner under-standing allows us to lay an all-important foundation for the structure of our life from which we can perceive and take the right avenues.

Fear comes from uncertainty; we can eliminate the fear within us when we

Chinese Gung Fu, 1963

know ourselves better. As the great Sun Tzu said: "When you know yourself and your opponent, you will win every time. When you know yourself but not your opponent, you will win one and lose one. However, when you do not know yourself or your opponent, you will be imperiled every time."

Jiddu Krishnamurti, the great philosopher who influenced Lee, said: "We must first understand ourselves in order to know anything and to understand and solve problems."

Self-discovery and understanding are part of the process of learning and growth. You should be constantly learning because life and experiences are your teacher. Education, learning and (physical) training should encourage you to question and search. With each new experience, you learn something new about yourself—whether good or bad. The self-help material available today is invaluable for developing yourself and opening doors to the acquisition of knowledge about yourself. By developing self-confidence and honing a deep will, you not only will be able to know yourself as a martial artist but also will be aided in your everyday life.

By having a greater understanding of yourself, you will be able to recognize those areas of your life and your art that need to be improved. You will be able to recognize your weaknesses and strengths. You will be able to know others and have faith in yourself when obstacles get in your way.

Lee was an astute philosopher. His art, *jeet kune do*, was one of the paths through which his life revealed its secrets. For other martial artists, it can be a means by which they can understand themselves. Lee said that the important thing for him was to understand himself while using his body. That's why his physical arts and philosophy are interrelated and inseparable.

Tao of Jeet Kune Do, 1975

If you want to gain a true understanding of Lee's philosophy—which can no doubt enrich your life—it is imperative to peer into the mind of this great philosopher. It is essential to study and read his works to gain a better understanding of him; only then can you absorb what is useful and fully appreciate what Lee was trying to say.

Bruce Lee's Fighting Method, 1978

Other products from Black Belt Books

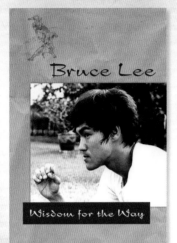

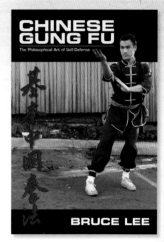

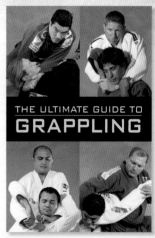
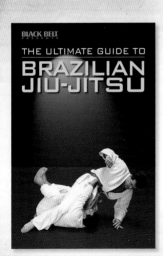
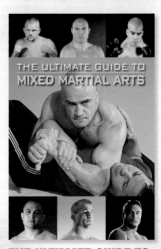